I0464030

Basics Preparation/ Understandings Before Establishing Business and Project Report

Basics Preparation/ Understandings Before Establishing Business and Project Report

How to establish the business

CA Sachin Gandhare

PARTRIDGE
A Penguin Random House Company

Copyright © 2015 by CA Sachin Gandhare.

ISBN: Softcover   978-1-4828-5797-9
             eBook   978-1-4828-5796-2

All rights reserved. No part of this book may be used or reproduced by any means, graphic, electronic, or mechanical, including photocopying, recording, taping or by any information storage retrieval system without the written permission of the author except in the case of brief quotations embodied in critical articles and reviews.

Because of the dynamic nature of the Internet, any web addresses or links contained in this book may have changed since publication and may no longer be valid. The views expressed in this work are solely those of the author and do not necessarily reflect the views of the publisher, and the publisher hereby disclaims any responsibility for them.

Print information available on the last page.

To order additional copies of this book, contact
Partridge India
000 800 10062 62
orders.india@partridgepublishing.com

www.partridgepublishing.com/india

Contents

Introduction

The book is basically designed to make people aware about their strength and its applicability in the business. The book increases the overall understanding of the business to everyone. It is a psycho social and practical approach to establishing a business., a novice can also read this book and have a good idea of business.

This book serves as a assistant to a person trying to enter into the business, it encourages peoples do the business and tries to make them a good businessman, it develops a sustainable inside in the mind of the individual by making him aware about problems, advantages, psychological and other aspects of the business, it helps to make the solid base and background for establishing business.

When we start thinking about our career,we always think about either of doing a job or the business i.e. whether to do the job or doing our own business, basically we have started thinking about our liking towards career. The process begins in standard 10th and we became serious in standard 12th, we see our future life as a very fruitful and satisfying. At this age we could also understand the importance of money in life, Therefore the basic expectation from our career is definitely the money i.e.

to fulfill the basic needs and little bit of luxury. To put it diplomatically enough money to meet expected needs of future.

Our parents and seniors always told us to work hard and to choose the job of our interest so that we could have the job satisfaction in our life. One must remember that a person has to perform many different work /roles in his life, it is not possible to derive satisfaction from every aspect of life like marriage, children, luxury etc. hence one should have at least career of his own choice.

The next foremost thing we expect is the job satisfaction which is a very important. Yes we have heard lot about it. Novice may not imagine or feel it properly, generally it is observed that earning money is more important for beginners than job satisfaction but later when they have earned enough money the job satisfaction is great concern for them and then they might think of changing the business line or job as they are not satisfied with same.

Understanding the Basic of Business.

What is a business?

Business: - It is something which is different from job. It is trading, manufacturing and providing services to society with a motive to have profit otherwise it is charity.

Now I tell you that there are two types of business, one which is intellectually difficult and another is practically difficult. They both have their own dynamics of estimated return, expected time and growth rate.

The examples of intellectually difficult business are book writing, Publication, Networking Company such as Face book, Whats up etc. The practically difficult businesses are Trading, Builder, Spinning Industry, and Textile Industry.

What is more satisfying is naturally the intellectual one because it gives you a beautiful felling. But the talent is also subject to demand, for example every one of us knows many cricket players by their name, but does we aware of our hockey players also. Both require the same talent level but cricket players earn more and hockey players less because people are more interested in watching cricket than hockey.

So according to ambition of individual and expected requirement for money and other luxury in life defines the choice of profession he will make.The money stands for confidence in the real world if you have enough of it, it will allow you for taking risk. No matter money is a very important thing of life.

So before spending the money, always think upon what future impact it will make, generally a person take a reverse approach firstly he secure the future of his family by taking the life insurance then go for the educational security of their children then go for gold for wife. In this way, he got himself locked in the circulation of money, so remember same should not happen in your life.

Basic Preparations expected

First step to do business in any sector begins with studing the region and understanding the nature and composition of industries in the region, it will give you brief idea about the opportunities available and the market of your region where you planning to manufacture and sell the product.

I must make clear that if you are a student who did not have any work experience, is highly recommend to do the job in the industry, It you want to go for the project, it is necessary to do the job. In this way you can understand basics like how accounts are managed,what is sales trends, what are production details,what are the marketing strategies, Fiancing strategies,administration etc.

By working in the various department your questions receives answers, You must try to understand the expense part and marketing part of the business. Try to develop your maturity level in the business by working close to boss.

If you confident enough and still think you should start your own business and you are matured enough to starts it, so start the work from Zero i.e. without availing finance from bank and other person. Initially start alone and if needed enter into partnership on clear understandable terms.

While investing for your future try to invest in the agriculture land where industrial N.A. is possible because doing the industrial NA is a very tedious job, so it is better to take your documents checked with NA authorities like town planning and metro departments,so that you can understand that where your dreams can be fulfilled with that propsed site.

Let's began on how to go for the business

The first step began with the setting up of mind and by reading these types of books.

The basic problem with life is we do not go for proper financial planning. We do have our family doctors but don't have family chartered accountants. Now a day the people act arbitrary and follow the street advice which is very dangerous, it is just like the taking the prescribed medicine from the chemist without any prescription.

Many times people approach to a non qualified CA or a non experienced person to get their ITR filed and ask them to file ITR without any tax liability. They usually charge then between Rs 100 to Rs 300.The person goes in the bank asking for some loan, the Bank officer laughs at him because he also understood that the return is prepared only to fulfill the formality and the same are also not appropriate according to loan requirement of the client.

The bank officer ask him certificate of chartered Accountant. Now he cannot go to CA,because he feared that CA will sign it or not. Then he again go for the same person who had filed his ITR and ask him to arrange the signature,he again charges him Rs.1000 and arranges the same.

The client had to pay ultimately 1500 and the ITR is also not according to the requirements so he won't get the benefit for what he deserves. If he earlier approached to the CA and revealed him about his need and requirement and financial obligation and investment expected in the near future. He could have got his financial document depicting the true and fair position of his financial affairs.

So it is seriously advised to visit the practicing chartered accountant so that you could keep your records in the proper manner and according to your future requirement of running your own enterprises and there are many chartered accountants who are specialized in the practice related to the consultancy of project financing and management consultancy.

The next step is to find a good project financing and management consultants

Dealing with expert /Consultant

<u>Getting services of expert for establishing business:</u> -

The people with multiple skill and knowledge could have their business established as the consultancy firm. They provide services to the people having resources to start the business. The clients may be lacking in skills and knowledge and having fear for entering in to the business.

A full time practicing professional can be great help to you and he could educate you about certain basic which you might does not know, there is a famous proverb that "good start is a half Done" so if you start with some good professional, which you find your are comfortable to discuss with can be a great help in your business.

The consultancy firm could help them by actively and passively contributing in the project. For example a person being is having the few acres of land in prime location which could be used for establishing a collage or school. Another person a layout owner has a Public Utility land in a particular city and problem is legally, it is not possible to sell it, it can be only given to lease to NGO or person for using it for Public Utility business.

The consultant could suggest you what type of projects could be established at your project site and also the availability of various subsidies for projects.

Hiring the professionals

A learned professional is a very much demanded by the people,the role of professional like chartered Accounts,Cost Accounts is increasing day by day, people think that hiring a Chartered accountant is a very costly job as compared to consultancy service required by businessman. But my friend I must tell you that in a company who employs chartered accountants have a number of small subsidiary and ancillary company whom they want to manage,you will be surprised to know a multinational company is a agglomeration of around 200 to 300 companies. In a big multinational organization whose names we listen in our day to day life do have almost 2000 to 3000 companies and firms as a subsidiary under their mother firm, this is called Holding Company and subsidiary company. The professional are hired to manage the smooth operations between these firms and to manage the interfirm transactions.

Now a day chartered accountants are providing such services to the small clients which were only demanded by big organization like strategic planning. It depends upon the complexity of services required by the client and the requirement of intervention demanded.

If you are going to some expert for the guidance for the project then you must ensure that you are paying him good enough for all kinds of expenses including the legal and other expenses for getting project executed.

People are more demanding such professional and offering then good remuneration for the quality and speed of consultancy delivered by them, the future of professional practice is such type of consultancy.

The following types of questions must be taken care of.

- We must first ask him about what type of project he has practical experience of establishing and working.
- What are financial requirement of the projects.
- The amount and percentage of bank finance available.
- Subsidies available.
- What are the collateral securities required by the bank for financing the projects. Remember at the time of starting this books the collateral securities requires were between 50 to 100 % and after finishing this book it has gone to 100 to 200 %. The banks are facing hard time and credit shortage

From here onwards your mind will be in obsession o f doing the business and he will starts non-stop thinking about what will going to happen and what should we do now. So in the mean time you must develop the following basic understanding about the business

History Of business

Business is commonly understood as trade /commerce. Earlier the business is done in the form of barter system. As there was no currency in use, something is exchanged of other for example Rice in exchange of Wheat and Animals in exchange of Metal etc.

A farmer who has cultivated rice might exchange it for vegetable oil and oil merchant may exchange it for other commodity. One could imagine that what types of difficulties could have happened to find right exchange,

To answer the problems Trader evolved as a person who could search for exchange. Because it is not possible to search every one,now please think this middle person he has to keep writing record for what quantity the Rajesh is having and what are his requirement and likewise Suresh, Mustafa and so on,

Suppose Rajesh came to market with rice and want to go back to village before night turns out. Then he approaches to the merchant/ broker for exchange so what does he do, he will buy cheap from him and provide him the right exchange of what he is looking for or he may promise him to get it delivered at his door step tomorrow morning and could make profit. This merchant or trader is turning out to be the businessman as he is buying cheaply and selling costly to others. These traders use to travel around the world for selling their stuff in appropriate marketplace.

In this way after studying the demands of the people coming from a particular village which is supposed to be Narkhed and as they have cotton to sell for and need cows in exchange so he will already arrange cow before cotton season by buying it in lot and at cheap rate, Now as he understood demand and supply and he wants to achieve economy in operation and proper management and administration of his business,he will keep employee and business will grow.

As the business grows the problems of records keeping will grow.To keep records of debtors and creditors he will issue them the hand written credit note and debit note for keeping record of there account and balance. He can also issue the promissory note or letter for credit or hundi for settling the account balances. The record kepping was very cumbersum and difficult to handle until the advent of currency which had made it easy by giving the measuring base.

I will like to tell you the interesting story about the negotiable instrument, the person coming to the market of Nagpur for selling the goods worth of Rs IIacs. He wants to leave for home but there is forest in between Nagpur and his village in Jabalpur. He might be at great risk as he carrying such a huge money so he approaches to Moneylender for drawing and negotiable instrument which could work like an cheque so he gets a hundi in the name of a moneylender i.e. an moneylender at the Jabalpur so he carried a piece of paper and code word which could be used at that location for getting money paid against that paper so the seller could gets his money paid in his village or the instruments can be sold to others for some exchange they charge some interest and other incidental charges for the same, this had developed a sense of trust between the parties and the system was so easy and efficient that it is still carried today people commonly known as Banking. The system had laid the foundation stone to the banking sector.

Basic Characterstics of businessman/ businesswomen: -

The attitude is very important in the business; the person with family background does come to business at early age. Sometimes people do try to do the job at someone else enterprises, just to prove themselves, they may even go to some other town for doing the same so that no one knows them.

Others are the people who don't like the job and have an attitude towards doing business they want to be a businessmen or the professional, they seriously don't like to work for others, and this type of class is a very innovative and much matured for doing the business.

There is another class basically in the marketing executives who has done marketing in their middle age and now they wants to shift to their own business. As they know that what time, energy, money and motivational levels are required to place the product in the homes/offices of people. They also understood the importance of Brand values, with their accumulated knowledge they can start a business.

Job Satisfaction and business

What business should we do? So for the same you need to understand your strengths and weaknesses, and how you're going to use then,

When a person is of 16 years old he/she seriously thinks about doing the job or business. In the collage we were having the idea and perception about the job. We understood that it may be a few hours business, in between 10 to 6 with no botheration afterword.

Does we have ever thought ever that we have to handle the mood of boss? We become dependent upon the job for our expenses and liabilities of Marriage, children's, parents, and activities of leisure.

In our society the success is always measured with wealth. The rich person gets a good life partner, home, car and various luxuries of life. Everyone wants everything quickly i.e. within few year of setting the business or getting the job. We feel pride to demonstrate the people what type of talent we have. Our idea of life is simple, earn more and spend more.

But after establishing ourself, some where we started felling that we are not satisfied with what we are doing.

To put in some simple words, job satisfaction could not be same for everyone, it may be more or less different for others, but it can be felt by every one of us in many ways.

"In my view when we feel satisfying about our job is when the job reflects our attitude our personality and our abilities, justifying our capabilities, a chance to uplift our learning our goal in our life and acts as mission we want to pursue in our life"

What will happen when we do not have satisfaction in work? Will it affect our personal and professional life?

What is people's definition of a satisfying career?

The following points must be considered which are expected from career

- Lot of opportunities for growth
- Health and well being
- Meaningful
- Reflection of our abilities and projections of our capabilities
- Remunerative
- Suitability to our personality and opportunity and appropriateness to our attitude.

The problems of dissatisfaction

- Increase in Job absenteeism
- Depending more on other satisfaction
- Substance abuse

- Stress and other psychological problems
- Decrease in performance, unable to produce desired result.

Reason behind dissatisfaction

Have you thought about the route of such problems, the basic root is human mind. Now a day's jobs are so demanding that you have to keep your mind literally available, attentive, and workable that you have to give the quick response to your boss demand? Remember the boss only like that employee who understands his style of work and adjust accordingly.

So ultimately our mind needs to stand in attention for12 hours and never relaxed because boss can demand your attention any time, this literally make you slave of demands and your creativity got killed in this process. If you are felling the job dissatisfaction for longer duration it may invite the heart related diseases, and substance abuse.

The serious problems of dissatisfaction:-

The human being are guided by satisfaction,that is the reason why we go to temple /mosque /gurudrwara and dissatisfaction is the problem of life,it causes the other effects like day dreaming, and mind blocking

It is a very natural phenomenon that if we face some problems our mind starts thinking about it until the problem is solved. Continuously thinking about the problem may create a phenomenon called mind block i.e. we cannot think about other things except a particular problem. In future it may affect our creativity badly.

When we are busy doing other things like Work,watching movie,spending time with the friends, we might automatically recalls thinking about the problems we are struck with (unsolved). This literally irritates our mind.

While relaxing or when we are alone, our problems block our mind and in order to avoid or ignore the same we use try diverting our mind, but diversion of mind is a temporary solution as it does not solve our problems. The diversion can be dangerous if it leads to some substance abuse like Cigrates, Tobacco, Drinks and others.

In this phase of our mind, we are just doing work as qualified labor. We will be unable to apply our abilities in work. The boss will notice the same and he will also pay us like a labor and we lose career opportunity,

In every field or sector you may find both types of job. Either monotonous or creative and autonomous. The companies generally go for the job enrichment and job rotation for maintaining the memento of employee.

The job is not a easy thing, it may be easy at clerical level but as the level increases the political influence,competition among the collage and unrealistic demands of boss,all these leaded to work related stress,which ultimately lead to substance abuse (smoking,drinking) and heart diseases,which could cost you a lot

Don't worry it's not too late for our own business.

If you want to have your own work place, want to work accordingly to your style and at your time. Where your abilities are truly disclosed and your capabilities can be enhanced, it is the business.

A businessman can enjoys a good social life and he finds time for everyone,

The golden rule

There is no retirement age in the business and one could get expertise in the few years only. The business could only take care of your every expectation about life and it's not a boring thing.

The social benefits of the business are truly a lot

In my case what had appealed to me that by not doing any job I am letting other person to have that job. By this way I am taking the efforts in the reduction of unemployment of my country by setting up a business.

I could decide my working hours of work, I can do the job as per its requirements. Now it is not important that I should always sit on my chair. I am not answerable to all my moves during the day. Remember these small things can make a lot of difference in your life

By doing business you can provide the employment to other person and in this way you can help other by giving them livelihood. In India the major reason of unemployment is not due to non availability of opportunities but due to inability to take costly education and due to poor condition of family they need to go to the work at an early age,and due to social custom they require to get married before properly settling at their life.

The ladies who have sacrificed their work life for the sake family betterment can also do business and justify their abilities. There are many ladies who are become the role model for others and achieved a remarkable success in their field of business.

The philosophy

Working for yourself is the way of life which could taste you freedom. Using the karma yoga as a way of life and for achieving salivation is also a way to pray the God. I must say working for contention is karma yoga. If you are not satisfied you can't make others happy and satisfied. Therefore one must work for his satisfaction.

Earlier all the people were working for themselves but now we find lot of population working for others and feeling unsatisfied with their life, because they are punished and insulted for their mistakes.

I would like to quote Mahatma Gandhi here

"Freedom is not worth having if it...Does not include the freedom to make mistakes... the best way to find yourself is to lose yourself in the services of others ...live as if you die tomorrow. Learn as if you were to live forever...you, just be the change you wish to see in the world ...An ounce of practice is worth more than tones of preaching"

The personality development is very easy with the business, because you also get the time for the same while doing business, we can go for other things to learn.

Employment is the monotonous job certain services are like doing few activities in your entire life

Now a day's governments job at the officer cadre demands for a very high level of commitment and hard work. They are not just for monitoring the work but the actual responsibility of executing the same. The clerical jobs are reducing because of advent of the computer technology.

Many organizations had stooped keeping the clerks, now they require the person who can feed the data to the computer for processing.

Earlier all the people were working for themselves because there were no organized sectors but now we find lot of population working for others as the sectors are getting organized. Sometimes we have feeling for employment like slavery. But same could be changed in the business.

The personality development is very easy with the business, because you also get the time for yourself who can be used to learn the new skill and enhancing the present skill. It's like gearing yourself physically and mentally.

Time Management guide.

The very important thing in the life, when you have time, it must be invested in planning the future work. When you are blessed with some opportunity you must be ready to justify the same.

Everything begins with the time management, the time management is required to break the incubation period and update the earlier learning with new learning. It's for updating your vision.

This is the very important factor in everyone's life that how to manage the time to make our dreams came true. There are various books and material on time management is available in market for study.

The time management is needed to proper utilization of our abilities. The time management is needed to have vision of what we are dreaming.

First in the day dreaming time we have to dream of doing the business and then try to make friends who are successful businessman, try to visit business you want to start, create a relationship with the professional like CA and project management consultant who could tell you a lot about project. The complete study is required to build your confidence in the business.

What is more important is how you organize yourself. Therefore you must learn and understand the every aspect of business.

There are certain indicated techniques to practice the time management, the time management means allotment of time to what you desire. That is to control time to turn results in your favor and that is too without disturbing your responsibilities.

Everything starts with the planning

1. Keep a diary to record your daily schedule
2. Use Smartphone as a working tool
3. Keep an watch on how you spend your time
4. Set priorities and targets according to your important
5. Organize yourself
6. Delegate your authority
7. Allow quality time to planning and high priority task
8. Do not allow other to waste your time.
9. Multitasking to be handled carefully.

There are two types of work

1. Field work
2. Table work

If you do the field work only you may find it easy as you have to operate in one mind set and same applicable for the sole table work too. If you try to mix up both of then, it will get difficult. As you have achieve targets for both which makes it very difficult. This is due to the fact we have to use different mindset for both and also need to operate in different physical settings which is difficult.

And if you are doing some creative table work then things becomes very difficult, but practice can make you perfect and remember a successful person is a personality of this kind i.e. one who is capable of managing both the areas (field and table) and stay creative all the times. The percentage of creativity in deed represents your development in command over execution of work.

For your personality development try to do creative work for at least one hour a day, if you could stay creative for at least an hour it will change your life. To live a creative life is ingenuity and intelligence way to live life

A person may think positively and creatively while he is busy and other may need a cool and calm place to think about his work. You can check this by watching some successful business that are continually keep themselves busy to keep their mind in good working condition, while other are sitting in cabin and doing their job, so no one could suggest which style is better. As it is an individual choice.

You should try to manage your priorities of thoughts, what issues are more important and when to think about it, you may sound it strange but practice it and see the benefits. You can try yoga.

Remember the health mind work better in healthy body the better is to try to do some physical workout to start thinking. One must use internet to get more and more understanding about the business you are planning to do.

To set the practical plan

Morning – exercise
Day – office
Evening – walking playing with children
Night – reading eating sleeping
Sunday, Saturday a different schedule
Try to identify small work and big work, small things like gardening, washing clothes, dusting taking pet in walk etc can be a good recreation. A morning walk is a better time to think about your important assignment and important planning. Try Yoga or some, outdoor game for mental alertness. Swimming is a better option.

In day time (12 to 3) try to do some routine work so that you can handle phone calls and other queries of office and people and delegate the routine work like paying bills, banking transactions, printing books of accounts.

From 3 to 6 after days lunch try to do field work. It will add to your learning as you can discover new thing, meeting new people.

From7 to10 you should do some mental thinking make strategy in light of days experience write a diary and your work problems and strategy at job,

10 to 12- forgot everything tries to relax, watch movies and discovery channel so that learning will be maximize, try to do some recreation activity.

Remember: - Every individual on the earth have only 24 hours to work and recreation, what makes a difference is how you utilize the same.

The problems and solutions while entering into business

First understand your expenses of life

- The basic problem with life is to what the problem is?
- Life is not but a lot about money, Generally, when the person want to starts his own business,he has to face a problem that his present lifestyle with the family is having an expenditure around Rs 30,000 to Rs 50,000 per month and he wants to have income of the same amount in upcoming project which do have his own gestation period,
- Every business has its own gestation period which may last till 2 years. This may be the time required to match the current status of income level. And basically your spouse is not ready for such experiment and she/he will do everything to stop you form doing something else from your present status, although there might be few exceptions. So it may take time for you take your spouse in the confidence.
- The breakup of expenses is as follows
- Household expenses: - 10000
- Installments: - 20000

- Car installments 15000
- Insurance policies 10000
- Other luxury 10000

  the last fact in this context are the people find their own ways, like asking spouse to ask her father to make will for property transfer and handover some land or property. And by using the same property they may plan to start business.

- Management of time is managing a balance between all responsibilities and priorities and it is very important otherwise you may have problems and you land yourself in crises.

- *Family relationships:* - The same may get affected due to increased priorities in your life, starting your own business and might need to scarify of your family time. You must convince and develop an understanding with your family and life partners so that their must not be any misunderstanding.

- Those people who have salary in the 5 figure will face strong resistant from their family and relatives. They will not to be allowed to leave their job initial phase of starting up business.

- The problems of paucity of time can be managed by delegating authority to the assistant. Definitely a person can hire someone who could manage their business work. This will reduce the pressure on you. If your employees are efficient and act according to your directions can bring the phenomenon results within a short span.

- If you spouse is not working then try to bring her into the business so that she will also be engaged and you could manage your business in better manner.
- You may not be supported by friends and well-wishers as you are going on different. It were observed that generally people resist the change. The change might be for their own benefits, but still people are concise about the change and do not welcome it.
- Therefore people in your vicinity circle may advice you to not to go for the business.

I am telling you an example of my child hood when I was planning to study business I asked my father to allow me to do so, he said ok. But after some days he came to me and said that it is very difficult, you better go for government jobs. As I asked him for the reason he said "lot of people have tried and failed and I was discussing the same in my office and people said that you should ask your child to choose other careers and so I am asking you to go for some other options". I was very surprised about his concerns.

I have asked him a simple question that the people you have consulted do they have their own business. He said none of them have their own business and either they are working in government offices or private. I said when they themselves have never done business how does they know about its success and failure and on what basis they are advising you. He was amused by my reply and allowed me for studding business.

- So this is the problem every businessman without family background. It is not so as far as business family concerns rather they give proper training from childhood and try to mould him in to a good businessman.

Incubation Effect

This is the terms used with the scuba driver. The scuba diver has to spend few days in the incubation chamber when he comes out of sea after spending few hours inside sea. They might require going into deep sea for some repair work of pipeline or for making documentary film or research on the sea bed. How long they have to stay in incubation chamber is depends on at what dept of sea they were working and how much time they have spend there, have you ever thought why it is so? Please check the internet for further details.

The reason for giving above example is that the same effect is also applicable to a person who is shifting to business after spending few year in service. In the same way if you do job and now you want to change the same too business and vice versa, the same incubation period you will take to adjust with new environment.

But the people travelling in the Vessel do not go though the incubation effect because the vessel protects them from sea pressure. Therefore if your new job/ business are very much similar so old one then you may require less time to adjust for the same

The effect of job on the personality

The job usually a part of our life and what activities we do most of the day is also responsible for making our attitude towards the people and it starts affecting our personality and life, for example A detective after doing few year of service may develop an attitude of suspicion towords many people. Following are certain observations of peoples on the job.

Monotonous / Dull Services/ jobs

After some years they find the job most irritating because having very less work to do, they donot know how to pass time without doing anything.

But they have other benefits like a good salary which covers the cost of living. If such a person plans to leave a job and to do the active business then it will be increase in the responsibility for him and if he is a government employee then rules does not allow him to do any other job/business during the service period,

They are actually became the non active person i.e. the person knows that he need not do anything more to get his bread and butter. His stigma for hard work is now ended and he gets used to easy life, but what he feels bad about his status, that he has not left with any challenge in his life, the job is not challenging and he cannot do anything to change the same because he has his own family expenses to be taken care off.

To establish a business as a means of livelihood will be very difficult for him due to social processing of his mind,the people with whom he spend time may demotivate him from business and divert his mind towards present job. Either he require strong will to change his destiny or wait for retirement.

It was generally observed that the government employee after retirement prefer some agricultural based business, it may be due to their old desire of doing business.

Active Jobs

Now in present scenario the professional who are not finding their job satisfying and getting annoyed due to unrealistic expectation. They were always in search of new job and business opportunities. The person who wants to leave the job and wants to start their own business can find this book very useful.

Professionals

The professional are the persons like doctors, CA,Consultants and others who are having their practice. These persons can easily shift to the business. The business could be share trading,writing the book or article,teaching and could be joining the family business.

Professional came into the profession due to their love for profession and after mastering in practice for 5 to 6 years they go for some other business it could be a very creative like music,writing painting, trading, manufacturing and other business.

For a **working professional** there are very few option left, generally the marketing persons comes to think of the business because they have the years of marketing experience and ability to learn and understand the marketing aspect of business. The easiest way to do business for then is to take some agency or franchisee of some company.

The problems associated with such agency is that, they pay you in percentage of sales which is very less and there is also responsibility for recovery of sales process dings, it is a very hectic job and profit are only for who are willing to go for big targets of sale and for the same they need secure the credit risk for recovery.

Freelancers

Not require to mention that they are looking for opportunity to earn. He can turn himself in to a good businessman.

The Business and people

The earlier times the doctors were doing only practice,then the numbers of doctors have increased and many forced to do the job, as the number were going on doctors at the job was opening clinic in the name of his spouse who is also an doctor and spending the evening time in attending the hospital.

The same also happened in CA profession. Earlier few CAs were only in the practice then the number increased and new CAs to job. Then again they were shifted to business. Few might joining their client business as a partner or director or vice president, now a day's many CA are turned into a good businessman.

The same things happens with the teachers earlier they started teaching in the schools/collages then shifted to their business of tuitions, later they bought agricultural land as a investment and now looking for some business opportunity in that place.

It's very common for marketing executive to start some business of their own after spending few decades in some company. with their reach knowledge and bsiness peoples contacts, they can do well in the business.

There are various business communities in much state like Marwari and Gujarati who have travelled in various parts of the country and aboard. They have developed their business from small amount of money and their entire generations have worked hard to ensure the future of upcoming generations, their moral and confidence is admirable.

People are sending their children to very costlier institutions for getting educated and they feel that they may get high paid jobs,but it's not true, no one could developed you unless you are willing to develop so instead of paying Rs 10 to Rs 50 lacs in education. It's better to have business of your own.

Factor Influence the entry requirement of business

When we enter in the business there are various factor responsible,like age,gender,level of knowledge,experience lets evaluate them in the various ways,

<u>The age really matters?: -</u> It depends upon the nature of business for certain business age really matters, the business where money recovery is to be done by traveling around the age will matters, but not for all.

<u>Experience</u> :- There are certain business where marketing is very important, therefore the experienced people are in more demand, the really fact that we assume that the experience grows with the age so age criteria will be associated with the experience factors.

<u>Educational qualification</u> :- Now a days the qualification is really matters. Not specialize but basic must be there,but specialized knowledge like engineering,doctor, Chartered Accountant,Cost accountant and company secretary and some marketing experience helps you to learn and develop faster than others.

The basic fact remains here is that the person could not have the knowledge of all the fields required for business.

Particular level and depth of Knowledge and experience could not be earned in few days it might takes years. for compensating the same we require the eligible person as a employee or partners.

Status of organization

The importance of status of organization

Proprietorship, HUF, partnership, private limited, public limited

Proprietorship :- It gives freedom of decision making and very successful with small scale organizations,it give a way to fast decision making and quick adjustment according to needs and help to maximum utilization of available resources for business.

Sole Proprietorship:-

The sole- means the single and proprietorship means sole jurisdiction here, it is a very simple type of business organization, easy to understand and requiring less documentation to start. Generally people start the business in their own name or they take the registration in the spouse name (wife / Husband) or close relative. It can be started with small amount of capital.

Following are the main advantages

Easy to form:-

It is very simple and easy to form, No separate PAN number is required, easy to open a bank account in your own name and few transactions can be routed through personal bank account.

Only registration under laws (Gumasta, VAT, CST) are required depending upon nature of business. The documentation is common for all the types of business organization.

Tax Benefit: - As there is no separate PAN number is required one can file ITR in his own name, sec -44 AD and other section of income tax can be taken benefits of only if relevant condition are fulfilled. Taxable income will be charged as per income tax slab rate i.e. concessional rates for individuals, Unlike the partnership firm, and company which is subject to flat rate of tax which is 30 %?

Property: - One can own property of the business in his own name,

Easy to Manage: - It is easily manageable as the proprietor has direct control. The household members can also look after his business. Many laws which are applicable to other form of organization are not applicable to proprietor.

Problems Of proprietorship:-

Unlimited Liability: - the liability of proprietor and partnership is unlimited. It means in case of default made in the payment of liability (for example repayment of loan) then his personal property is subject to attachment for the repayment. To explain it further their personal assets will be sold to pay off their debts and liability.

Management :- The management is wholly depend upon the person and problems of his individual life can also affect his business,he find difficult to leave the business for personal reasons, as the proprietor he has to look after everything because keeping employee at every palace is very costly to him.

Suitability: - It is basically suitable for the small organization and beginner in the business. The legal problems/difficulties are there for conversion of proprietorship in to company. If in future you are planning to convert it into the public or private limited company then owner required to pay the stamp duty at applicable rate for the cost of assets transferred in the company name... The asset and liabilities are also required to be transferred in to the name of the company i.e. ownership rights of the propriters ends when assets are trnsferred in the name of company. Therefore it is better to consult the chartered accountants and other professional for resolving the matter.

HUF: - This is so popular because it is easy to form and enjoy almost all the benefits of proprietorship in terms of tax exceptions and other statutory advantages.

Partnership
Formation:-

Like proprietor, partnership can also be formed with very less legality. The legal registrations are applicable with increase in turnover/ sales of organization.

Before you start thinking of entering into partnership all the partners are expected to write down on a piece of paper what does they understands about partnership and it's working. The same understanding must be discussed with the professionals like CA and others so that all the queries will be taken care off.

The partnership deed acts as an instrument to reduce your understanding in writing and it is better to get it registered, because it is compulsory for VAT registration and Income Tax purpose and for availing the bank finance.

Resourcefulness

As partnership is done for sharing the knowledge,time and efficiency of the partners and to give more commitment to business,it is very desired that all the partner must provide their full capacity and efficiency and demonstrate their business acumen in the business,the partner can act as a substitute for each other,the vital and specialized experience of the partners can be utilized in the great extend.

Availability of large resources:-

Since two or more partners join hands to start a partnership business, it may be possible to pool together more resources as compared to a sole proprietorship. All the partners together can contribute more capital, more effort and more time for the business.

Better and quality decisions

The decision making is a quality thing in the partnership more partner can contribute their knowledge and better decisions can be taken.

Communication problems

But there is also the problems in communication between the partners, which could cost the business. lot of time wasted in the coordination efforts between the partners. They may be politics played by partners between themselves.

Risk sharing:-

The risk of doing business is shared, and also the problems are shared.

Problems: - the common problems faced by partnership firm are many. Problems might be with the sharing of loses, withdrawing of money. The problems may arise if unfortunately any partner dies, then it again becomes difficult to measure his share and handover the same to his widow and children's.

There is another very big problem is that the unlimited risk clause, due to which partners are jointly and severely liable for the acts of other partners and hence it bring the great risk and psychological pressure on each other's. To answer such a problems one can use LLP (Limited llability Partnership) for limiting his liability to the extent of his share.

Lack of harmony and lack of transparency is also the reason for difficulties of partnership, the certain law restrict the number of partner to 20 and so that is the limitation of their growth.

Suitability:-
It is suitable for the medium scale business organization.

Formation of company

The company is a bigger form of organization which has separate legal identity in the court of law from its members, it means it can own properties in its own name and can sue and get sued in its own name. The members could not interfere in its day to day operations, only the directors are authorized to transact the business.

Limited liability

The foremost advantages for which the company are most sought is that the limited liabilities. Which means that, In case of default by directors you will be liable for the companies' liabilities only up to your unpaid share of capital.

For example:-

If you have invested in the shares of the company and later it was discover that the company is going into liquidation and its assets are not enough to pay off all its liabilities. In this case also your liability will be limited only to the unpaid amount of shares procured by you. To explain it further your other properties will not be to be sold even if company is unable to pay of its liabilities.

This doctrine is not available to proprietorship, partnership and HUF.

Separate legal Entity

The company heve its own identity, It is trated as a individual person for all legal purpose. It can own asstes in its own name, It can file the law suit in its own name and can be sued upon in its own name. It can legally enforce its all rights against any person and have its common seal, the directors are as the agents of the company and they can be changed by the shareholders of the company.

Perpetual succession:-

The company is not a natural person so it cannot die and can't go for the retirement, the shareholders of the company may change due to share transfer, death and successions but the company will remain the same and will last forever unless legally liquidated.

The big companies like TATA, BIRLA have being founded by their founders about 100 years ago,but the companies are still there and doing their business even after the death of their founder.

Pubic limited:-

The major advantage of formation of public limited company is, it can offer its shares direly to the general public. It can also offer its shares through stock Exchange. This organization can tap the thousands of people for getting finance. The public limited company is mostly suitable if you are a large scale enterprise.

The best way is to try every way at right time

As you start the business it is better to start with the proprietary concern. After 1 year of experience you may go for the partnership and then try for the private limited and next step is to public limited.

Sectors of business

The business done in various sectors

1. **Old and well established sectors**
2. **Developing sectors and**
3. **Invented and future sectors**

Agriculture, Accounting, Auditing, Apparel and accessories, Automotive, Cooperative bank, Grocery, Health care, Services related to internet, Legal, Manufacturing, Movie making, Music, Publication and Newspaper, brokerage, biotechnology, pharmaceuticals, newspaper Publishers, cargo handling, publishing chemical, real estate, consulting, security and commodity exchange, consumer product, services, cosmetics, detergent and soap, software, departmental store, sports, education, technology, electronics, transportation and lot more.

Searching benefits for particular Industrial sectors

While planning for the business in particular sector we must understand it first. It is highly recommended that one should visit the website of the concerned ministry of the government. The websites of central,state and even local government gives you lot of information.

It provides you the first hand information on present trends of business and government assistance in the form of subsidy and others benefits available. The users must go for the official web site for the ministry and after studing the same you must to visit the local office of such ministry.

For example,

The website of food processing ministry may reveal the following,

Food Processing sectors ; like fruits and vegetables, milk/ meat/poultry /fish product,cereal /other consumer food products, rice/flour/pulse/oil milling and such other agro –Horti sectors including food flavors, colors,oleoresins, spices,coconut, mushrooms, wines and hops will be covered under the scheme. The activity of aerated water, packed drinking water and soft drink will not be considered for financial assistance under the scheme.

So one can notice fro above paragraph that the activity of soft drink and packed drinking water is not covered under the same although it comes under food processing industry. therefore you may end up doing the buiness which may not come under any gverment soponsered scheme.

The schemes are very good and alluring but it has its own practical difficulties. Subsidy available: - 25% to open category and 33.33% to SC /ST category. This is also subject to certain conditions.

There are other schemes like entrepreneur development program and other programs for service sector but what government expects from you is practically very difficult to get done.

so we must check a guideline for projects under national importance and subsidy in terms of applicability and the eligibility criteria.

Scale (Size) of business

The size is like small, medium and large then mega large and ultra large

The size is very important and with increase in size other factors do come in to play. If we are planning for small and medium enterprises it will definitely going to take 2 to5 labors for normal business where manual labor is not key important,and so we going to need one supervisor come manager. This could be the minimum cost one may incurers to do the business. There are certain labor laws which get in force with the increase in the capacity like ESIC & PF,WORKMENS COPENSATON ACT etc. And same going to cost us in terms of administrative cost. Now a days people are appointing their employees through the manpower consultant which is beneficial for most of employers

Problems associated with large organization :- There is no such upper limit for the rich persons, people does have so much money that one could never imagine. Due to such huge reserve of money they have a large power under their command, they could buy an organization in a matter of weeks. Therefore the public company which is listed on stock exchange always fear of hostile takeover problems and hence they try to make themselves unpleasant to hostile takeover by investing in various manufacturing and processing line.

Classification Industries

The dictionary meaning of industries means the organized action of people for making product and for selling it and earning profits

The industries are classified in terms of size location and sector,

Beside this for the purpose of their necessity they can be classified as follows

I) Basic and Primary –Industries: - These are the industries which are necessary for flourishing of other industries. the following products and industries are necessary for the purpose
    *   Power
    *   Mining of Coal, Iron Ore and other Mining
    *   Agricultural processing
    *   Infrastructure,rail road,airport

The above mentioned industries are the examples of primary sector industries which is necessary for the development of other industries. By mere reading of same one can easily understand the necessity and importance of this sector.

For ex: - If power tariff is very high in Maharashtra state then new and old units may shift to other states like Chhattisgarh. This could be the reason of shifting of new industries form Maharashtra to Chhattisgarh. This will also cause the loss of growth opportunities of in Maharashtra.

2) Secondary Industries :- These basic industries provides input to the other industries like steel industries, capital and industrial goods, factory equipments. These industries require high capital investments and a lot of manpower.

3) The third nature of industry is entertainment, cosmetics and service sector which is a fast emerging sector of Indian economy. the government is earning lot of revenue in the form of service tax from this industries.

4) The industries are also classified according to their size as small medium, large and mega large projects.

All the industries have their different position in the country's economy. before entering in the business you must understand the financial returns and socio –economic position of the business, future expected trends in the business and age of the industry.

Agro based Industries: - cotton, jute, silk, oil like sunflower, cotton seed and soyabins etc., tea, coffee

Industries based on minerals, chemicals: - petrochemicals and other chemicals, metal industries, fertilizers, cement, glass, drugs and pharmacy.

Forest based products: - Bidi Industries, paper industries, rubber industries, forest tourism.

<u>The Industries and Government</u>:-

The central government - It has made a separate ministry "Ministry of Micro, small & medium enterprise" which looks after the MSME sector, it's governed and helps them for development.

The government has played central role in the development of SME sector. The government of India is very serious about the development of SME sectors. It is biggest employer after agriculture sector which is very important for growing population of unemployed persons.

The government of India had made many rules like compulsory procurement of goods and services of MSME sector by government companies.

The government has created MSME as a separate ministry, which itself reveals the importance is given to SME. This is the most subsides sectors after the agriculture. It does take responsibility of socio-economic development in the country.

One could go to msme.gov.in/web/portal/new-default. ospx.On the left hand side of home page, you can find programs & scheme heading which will guide you to search engine and you can find a very convenient way to search for scheme and incentives related to the industry you are interested in.

There is a lot of information about various topics where one entrepreneur will be interested in. The interested person could explore the site to the maximum.

Stock Exchange: - In order to ensure the proper flow of finance to the MSME sector, the government had created a separate segment on stock exchange called SME exchange. This allows the SME sector to offer its shares to the public at large. Earlier these facilities are only available to large organizations.

The Industrial Policy of State:-

Beside central policy, there is state government who also interested in development of their state industrial portfolio as well as development of peoples skills.

The state government does make their industrial policy likewise the Industrial Policy of Maharashtra 2013 to 2018. This policy is vision of state and their development targets.

The most important things are employment for all and a fulfillment of needs of peoples. The state industrial policy ensures sectarian development in full swing and to eliminates or hurdles in the development.

The policy contain following points among the other

1. It explains about the state and its strength in terms of strategic advantage, quality of population, availability of labor, potential sources of raw material and availability of land and other natural advantages for setting the business.

2. It aims at developing the sector as a world class destination of business, with the targets of making the sate no. 1, global destination for industrial development.

3. It gives its focus on underdeveloped region of the state and put a greater emphasis upon their development. If you are interested in starting business in underdeveloped region you may have lot of benefits. The government now a day's giving lots of benefits to naxal hit region in order to develop them and to enhance the standard of living among tribal people.

4. It provides for tailor made i.e. customized package for ultra mega i.e. very big project. The project like setting up of manufacturing unit, mega manufacturing unit is always welcomed by the state as it provide lot of taxes and employment opportunities at large scale. The all states in India call them for setting up the large project in their states.

5. The government is very much concerned with MSME Micro Small and Medium enterprises as they are biggest employment provider after agriculture.

6. The policy of governments is initiative to encourage the industries which will leads to

employment generation. The employment generation is a need and social responsibility of the government as public elected them to take the social responsibilities and challenges.

7. It allows the investor to safely park its investment and fair return on investment. In practically the investor are the people who are interested in their investment return and not interested in doing business. The examples of such people are Banks, Financial Institutions, and shareholders.

8. The other types of investor are business people who are interested in actually doing business provided it should not be difficult enough to establish i.e. if the business requires certain numbers of NOC of concerned authorities and if they are very difficult to get due to red tapes, burocrats, interference and stringent compliance requirement... For ex. The NOC of Fire and town planning is will cumbersome in certain part of countries and takes long time to get.

9. The industrial polices is the road map for infrastructure development it announces the various SEZ, MIDC extension and announcement and various other development activities like laying railway siding in the industrial area, residential quarter for employees in the industrial areas, community centre, school, water treatment plant etc.

10. It takes case of sick unit for its revival or takes over by health units in order to maintain the

growth and to take responsibility of employees of sick unit.

11. The policy announces various incentives which are necessary and act as a booster for the industrial growth and development.

12. Various mechanization and modernization system are introduced in order to increase frequency and create an understanding among industrialist that the government is in favor of development. Various initiatives like skill development computerization and business process emergency are introduced and monitored.

13. It gives government interest and incentives for ultra mega project and it increases the competitiveness in the market, put a check on monopolies, promoters development and promotion schemes, marketing assistance scheme, skill development scheme, assistance for lean manufacturing scheme. Design assistance scheme, fiscal incentives to MSME. In Maharashtra the taluka/area are classified according to their developments. There are highest incentives for unit setup under naxalism affected area and no industry district. Details of subsidy can be studied under subsidy head. It gives seed money scheme. It helps in renewal of sick units by providing them loan at some percentage (for industrial sickness read the head of industrial sickness). It encourages green initiatives and technology up gradation. It strength district industries centre.

Subsidy:

The subsidy is like something people understood as the reward for the business they want to do, they thought that the subsidy as their right and they must get it before hand and before starting of business, but let me know you almost all the useful subsidy available are subject to sanction of your project loan by the nationalize/nodal bank please understood I mean project loan and not other loan like LAP loan i.e. like giving loan against your property it may be in form of cash credit or term loan, but you need to have the project loan sanctioned from the nationalized bank or bank approved by the subsidy giving authority and capital subsidy is paid by the government as a contribution in the form of repayment of monthly installments

Types:-Mainly there are two types capital subsidy, and interest subsidy, the capital subsidy is like presently 25 % to 33% of project cost. The most important point here is. If your account becomes NPA (Non performing assets in banking terms, it is the loan where the interest and installments are overdue) then your subsidy will be automatically stopped.

SME Sector
MSME role in India

The role of Micro, small and medium enterprises in the country development is lot. The SME are very crucial and important to the country economic and sociality, it is backbone of our county. It is the biggest employer of people after agriculture, the characteristics of SME is enumerated in the following way.

I. *Training Institute* :- Besides it is a biggest employers,it serves the needs of society as training centre,it gives the skills training to the people and also gives them a minimum bearable salary while they are getting training, generally it is observed that the boys/girls in their young age work here for learning skills and when they plan to have family they leave SME to join some large organization or they may even leave for the foreign country for better job opportunities. So it serves as a practical training institute in social scene

The people like welder,machine fitter,plumber and many others come to this sector for learning the basic working skills which also a practical training institute. It can create good entrepreneurs for the society.

It also helps the white collar employees to get training and working knowledge. In future these accountants,administration staff and management trainee may becomes the new class of entrepreneur and also gives their valuable contribution in development of relevant sector. Here people understands the commercial way of doing the things.

The MSME are the research centre which gives birth to many innovation on day to day basis, it gives many ways of cost saving and giving innovative solutions to the problems of the people like customers, employers and their co workers. it allows the entrepreneurs to show their innovative skills and technique to the world, it act as a platform to invention and innovation. If the reader's wants to set up the MSME, I will suggest him to visit few organizations dealing with the same product and service. It will make you aware of differences in approach and working culture.

Bridge between people and product:-

The MSME serves as a bridge between product and people as the owner of the same are in continuous liason with the customers they understand them better so they can make product useful and within budget of the people,it helps the people and give them custom made innovative product. It does support to those people who cannot afford the complicated and costly technology. it shows a cost effective ways of doing a particular thing which serves the purpose of people and reduce peoples dependence on the imported product and costly technology. It does helps nation to save valuable foreign exchange which otherwise be used for import of products and services.

TAILOR MADE PRODUCT : the MSME entrepreneur being in the great touch with the customers and able to spend time and energy on understanding their needs and requirement,it acts as a innovator of new product and new markets and new customer class,MSME entrepreneurs changes the perusal and taste of customers. It often noticed that the big organization then enter into same product or alike with an improved packing. It is the very innovative sector which provides the tailor made services to the people in a cost-effective way.

For ex:- Earlier period the cloths are made by hands and the handloom was used to make product, by invention of the power loom the handloom industry lost its growth opprtuinites and today the handloom industry is in very bad phase.

Better utilization of local resources

The MSME is helping the country to utilize local resources in an effective manner and it does utilize local material, local talent, local finance and locally available skills and techniques, so it gives importance to all locally available resources and ensure their effective use.

Social effect: - It provides means of life to people and stops migration of people from one place to another, it gives better employment opportunity and add to better standard of living of people and ensures their well being.

Business Economics

Economics is the subject which is very much ignored while understanding the project. It is also misunderstood with financial viability of the project, the economics here mean how you will shift from your present position to expected position without disturbing your financial obligations. i.e. how will you manage to move from the present position to the next desired position in a profitable way, if economy gets disturbed then you might required to face music.

Cost of development : - the development cost is the cost which we do not consider in financial planning but it is very important, the cost of development is as follows.

When we got the job we were unmarried and then we have ample money for ourselves and our needs, then we get married next we have children then we do have to make provisions for their expense and future.

Don't you think these expenses are our liability which we call in social terms responsibility

We start business we start it from rented premises, then our business flourishes and we go for additional staff and buy our own office premises, this is our development.

For example many of you have seen that people in prime location of market places do some retail business like ice cream selling and medicine store but if we take the notional rent of property in to consideration we may find that they are in loss. Then how could they survive?, because they are fully developed and they have no liabilities they just required money to meet there own personal and annual expenses with any agenda for development.

Cost of maintaining the present income:-

When we began the starts business sometimes the luck favors sometimes the bad luck favors but over a period of time we understand that there are also expenses and sacrifices for maintaining the present quantum of receipts.

Suppose we are doing the agriculture and during the 1st season we have earned 1 lac/per acre so does it means in next season we will earn the same amount. In order to maintain the income you have to add manures and fertilizers which were not required in the first year.

The basics of Business Economics

We have heard lot about economic problem and many readers might be reading this book in order to solve their economic problem and these types of books might solve it, as it provides necessary understanding to the reader about their dream of becoming businessman.

The economy is directly linked with efficiency. The greater efficiency achieves better economy. The word economics is a subject, which deals with study of economy. Basically economy is classified in 2 categories Micro and Macro

Micro: - Economy is wholly concerned with your pocket this micro economy deals with individual as a subject. It studies economy of an individual person. It does have social & psychological aspect of an individual person. It concerns socio- economic life of individual.

In electronic media we learn lot about farmer's suicides, which is due to mismanagement of their economic life. Farmer does not commit suicide when particular crop or season fail, but when he understood that in the future he will be unable to manage his economic well being and could not repay his debts and could not take care of his family and due to this frustration he commit suicide. So the non-balance & mismanagement of economic life may lead to modern day life stress and physiological problem which may lead to Cardiac and other physical as well as pysychological Problems.

Macro: - It is concerned with whole i.e. economic of nation, world, and state. The Macro economy deals with national GDP (Gross Domestic Product), National Income, National Expenses etc.

Macroeconomic entails studies which make us to understand exactly what we are doing with our income and wealth of our country. Even country have natural resources in form of Gold, Coal, Uranium, Diamond.

The economy tells what we are doing with national wealth and manner of utilization of same. How we are spending our national income. If we spend all our national income and feeding poor, providing subsidy then how does infrastructure development of our country could be achieved. We need to build infrastructure and empower employment generation.

The Government could not take bold step on reduction of subsidy, because it has its own social and political aspects. Therefore we have to manage our money and wealth in such a manner so that we can make social justice to people, social environment and mother earth also. We should achieve our economic surplus so that we can sustain bad days in future.

The purpose of studying Macro economy is effective utilization of available resources of Men, material, money and machinery in order to maximize wealth of nation to maintain steady growth of economy and to have control on inflation etc.

Every Country has a type of economic set up which are of 3 types. Socialistic economic (China), Capitalistic Economy (USA) and mixed Economy (India). For the interest of reader would like to elaborate it further in brief.

Socialist economy (CHINA) is the type of set up where the government own maximum or all resources and business and regulate every major aspect of economy like production, distribution, collection i.e. there is only one employer in the country which is government and total work force belong to government companies. The basic service motive behind this set up is the social interest of people and with the focus on social well being, justice and development of all people in equality. Only few sectors are opened for public, but all the important sector are controlled by government.

Capitalist economy (USA) is the type of economy which is assumed to be the sign of development of nation. Until now with the development of China it was assumed that development of countries is only possible with implementation of capitalistic economy. The characteristics of such economy can be assumed as follows. The role of government is like observer, controlling law and order and justice and to maintain healthy competition. But all the enterprises (Except few like military, police and nuclear bomb) are controlled by individuals. The market is a free market and no government control over factors like demand, supply, necessity and need. This economy ensures speed decision by companies as they are controlled by individual who are very professional in their approach. The top economies of world are capital economies.

Mixed Economy: - PPP,three P i.e. Public and People participation where government and individual come in of participation to excite all the projects, it is combination of government and private people. The price mechanism is free. This policy of mixed economy is very suitable for developing countries. Hence only some importance sector are fully owned by government. And other sector by private and in few sector the government and non-government participates i.e. individual / private enterprises are partners. This ensures health, market competition. This also provides due attention to social values. This is a liberalization of economy. In this set up the government is more focused on regulation than actually doing the business.

Economic Growth

The economic growth of country is very important you have heard of poor nation and wealthy nation. Poor families and poor nation find it difficult to feed its population while wealth nation are spoiling food. So while doing business in the particular place you must have to study the economic growth of state and people. In India we do have more than 25 states, but it is also truth they are all not homogeneous in respect of taxation and easiness of doing business.

The north-east part of nation is having very few industries parks, also in our Maharashtra only Mumbai; Pune is having lot of industries while Yavatmal and Gondia district is not having that much of industrial centre.

The economic growth is also associated with economic development and equality of growth is very important otherwise population migration will be high.

Earlier in my hometown Nagpur we are finding Chhattisgarh labors more in number, also labor from Rajasthan used to come here, but now as Chhattisgarh has become a fast developing state and we are facing labor problem in Maharashtra.

The economic growth must be understood in terms of every aspect. Its trends of growth must be understood in order to have sound planning about industry you want to establish and you must study the impact of economic trends on individual and industrial growth.

We must plan our business according to growth trend because growth trends and selling of particular goods have a direct link. So we must understand the future benefits of doing a particular business.

The economic development is can be understood by following example. Earlier there was no road between 2 cities, the people used bullock cart which took 10 days to travel and transport, but with the railway journey had reduced this time to 1 day. This is economic development it is more concerned with poverty reduction, infrastructure development, structural charges etc.

The economic development is of 3 types, Undeveloped, Developing & Developed Economy.

For the sake of interest we can read the what undeveloped, developing and developed economic are early saying a foreign countries like Zimbabwe and few other like Afghanistan are underdeveloped, India is a developing economy and Japan, France & USA are developed economic. By reading the mere example one can easily understood what the basic differences are considering the means and stand point of development.

Why we study development is because the different types of goods and different quality level are demanded with the development of economy. If in Afghanistan you will ask someone to buy BMW and AUDI, he won't be ready for same i.e. to say you will find no customer for same. In UK and USA it is very common to own such vehicle.

The Expensive watches, dress, and ornaments will be available in big market i.e. developed places. The agro – based and basic raw materials will be easily available in undeveloped countries. The agriculture output is majority of Gross domestic product (GDP) in underdeveloped and developing economies.

In other words, the under developed country will be a big market for Agricultural raw material while developed country is a big market for finished goods.

Therefore when we are trying to become industrialist we need to have understanding about level of development so that we can establish our business like wise.

For example: - The expenses Gems and expensive watches and other luxurious commodities will be sold in developed countries. Necessities and daily requirement good will be more demanded in other areas.

The average population will be wealthier in developed economics. Their purchasing power will be high. They will have good amount of money for their enjoyment and leisure activity.

There is lot of economics laws and means to calculate variables like per capita income and human development index and purchasing power parity Etc. one must try to understand basic knowledge of the entire subject that does affect the business.

One practical phenomenon I observed was that of trends, it means what is now happening in metro city will shift to non metro city after few year and then it will go to small cities and then to villages. This generally people understood as development. Generally businessman belonging to small cities visits the big city in search of idea for business.

Wealth management

The word management resembles here to the wealth management, remember when we are in school we were not worried about wealth. Things change when we become adult and understood the importance of wealth.

Everyone have some wealth which can be calculated in terms of money and everyone has his own monetary requirements, let's go by one example suppose you have a loan of 20 lacs and when you have received a sum of Rs 1 lacs and such receipts are not frequent. Then at first instant you might think of loan repayment but you may go for buying some gold or plot of land in remote area which is expected to give double the price after a span of 10years and this is wealthy management

What is business environment?

What is environment in the business term means, it is nothing but the dynamic conditions under which the business operates, the following points will elaborate it clearly

Political environment:- If the political ruling party is having majority in both the houses the execution of development work becomes very fast if the state government and central government is under same party then the opportunities for development Is bound to increase. This is called the win win situation if political party make nurturing environment i.e. favorable credit policy,interest cut rates on credit, and making policies to ensure stable growth, all around development of nation etc. the opportunities for growth are seriously affected by political will.

Labor problems:-

In our country having a population of 1.25 billion in which majority is youth, but still it is difficult to find the industrial labor. Every businessman is frustrated due to labor problems.

Contract labors:-

The bigger companies are facing problems due to labor absentee and number of labor laws to deal with which requires HR department to deal with labor issue and this increase the administrative cost of companies. Therefore in order to answer the aforesaid issue the companies prefer the appointment of contactors for supply of labor.

By doing so, nothing will be changed but instead of keeping labors on company payroll they put them on the contactor pay roll. The employee even after working for 10 to 15 years doesn't gets any benefits like PF, Pension and so on. It was actually noticed that there are lot of violent clashes between management and these employees over the job related benefits and pension.

The contract labor does not have the job security and no retirement benefits form the company. The contact lobar problems are becomes worse in many company as they are faced a long litigation in court and their manufacturing units are closed for a long considerable time which had affected their production targets and customer management badly.

The availability of labor at reasonable cost acceptance level is an important thing in the business

Government Policies

The government policy means how much the government favoring the business in present, the agenda of all the parties ruling the country is to develop the business and to benefit the businessman, but will they able to do so is another thing. The vision of government very important and the ability to implement the new reforms is utmost necessary.

A general policy is always declared for the SME sector which explains the government stand on various issues and what are the benefits they are providing to the SME sector. It does also declared the various subsidy to the new business and benefits in the operation and other benefits they are providing to the individuals and SME sectors. The amount of subsidy the government are passing is also important,the government also announces the programs of entrepreneur developments, the availability of seed finance the financing opportunities to new as well as existing business units.

Infrastructure facility: - the infrastructure has direct impact on business growth, popper transportation faculties ensure the labor availability, proper infrastructure through road connectivity ensures the good mobility of resources.

For example-

Now day's road connectivity is better which allows you to travel faster so that one can easily go to his factory 50 Km away and get back to his home at city in evening, the better infrastructure facilitated the growth of business in manifolds.

A railway siding development for SEZ and expansion of MIDC, better road,bus and railway connectivity and other communication facility made the doing business an interesting thing.

Understanding the Market

When we visit a market we can observe that the market is of two types one is retail sector and another is wholesale sector, but in the market the shops are situated near and close to each other, sometime during my childhood I was very surprised that how can be the same product is sold by everyone and why so much people are sitting at the same place.

Market / competition.

The market and competition can be correlated in some way or other. The market itself means competition. The nature of market & competition is different in different places.

There is no market without competition; the competition insures the better product and services at reasonable rates. The competition is desired by the customers. the business man wants to earn the profit and for the same they want to be ahead in the competition.

Before entering into any business, you must need to study the nature of competition, strength of the competitor and your patience and mental strength. The competitors sometimes form a cartel to prevent the entry of new player in the market. Sometimes the competitors even use legal/ illegal means to stay ahead in the competition.

How market is created: - the market may start by single person lets take an example of fruit merchant. He places his shop on the new location. (The location mean where he could be spotted by people). Then he sells his fruits to people. Due easiness and availability, the peoples get attracted to him and he earns exceptional returns. He is also observed by other fruits seller and they also place a shop beside him and market gets developed.

Now it will bring competition among the fruit sellers and they collectively will attract lot of customers, and as hundreds of people getting attracted to this small market will again increase the market as small market cannot serve large people in a small time span as the people expects services within the minutes. Due to the expectation of swift service by customers there is scope remains for new palyers to enter in to the market.

Their collective business will be observed by big seller like branded fruit seller and whole seller and they will also jump into competition. Then some attractive branded store will establish their stores providing better credit facilities and ambiance. To reduce the cost of oprations the Corporate may offer online services and vaiouse discounts to its customers.

In order to understand a business

    I.   Make friends of the same business

2. Observe a business for a year, you must understand the sales potential of every month during the year.

Following points may come to your mind

1. Skills; - how to sell the product.
2. What is the product
3. What will be the credit policy
4. What is the product life cycle
5. What is the recovery period
6. What are the government policies

What type of retunes are expected and when time the retunes are low and high.

How Market is driven? The markets are driven by many forces and factors which are summarized below.

1. Demand and Supply forces.
2. Preferences & taste
3. Level of competition
4. Needs & requirement
    a. Credit policy
    b. Safety & security
    c. Quality
    d. After sell price
    e. Regulatory authority

Regulatory authority :- It is like a regulator of market which are required to ensure customers safety, fare price, avoid unhealthy competition and ensures customer & consumer protection.

For Ex.:- Central Bank (R.B.I in India) :- It regulate credit market ensure cheap rates to borrower and boost infrastructure growth in the country.

IRAI – Regulator for mobile & telephone.
IRDA:-Insurance regulatory authority
SEBI – Regulator for stock market, share market.

Types of financing

The finance is the backbone of all enterprises. Financing means making funds available to enterprises whenever it required. The funds are required by enterprises for purchasing assets paying liabilities, purchasing raw material and day to day expenses. Finance is required by all businessmen. Everyone wants his business to be finance in a cost effective way. In our Maharashtra people heavily depends upon finance for establishing a new enterprises.

The finance is provided by following institutions.

The finance could be arranged by various means explained below.

Self financing: - The money can be brought from own source i.e. borrowings from friends and relatives. This kind of financing is desired when the gestation period is 3 to 5 years. The proprietorships and partnership firms generally use the same

Bank finance: - The banks do offer the finance to the people for Development, Expansion of business and to meet working capital requirements. The bank always ask for primary and collateral security. One must understand the difference between the terms like mortgage,pledge, hypothecation before availing the bank finance. The banks offers finance in the form of Term loan, Cash Credit Facilities, Bank Overdrafts, Letter of credit, Discounting of negotiable instruments and Bank Guarantee.

Nationalized Bank: - The banks like SBI, BOI, BOM, and UBI etc etc are very important in developing our nation. They providing a credit from small to ultra large project and make the country self dependent. These banks are very cooperative. These banks help a lot to all types of customers.

Commercial bank: - They do provide finance to all businessmen's and many of them are NODAL bank i.e. banks authorized by government to collect the amount of subsidy. Practically it is observed that these banks hesitate in financing in the rural areas.

<u>Credit co-operative banks: -</u> These are governed by committee. This is formed from capital of members with common interest, it is a general people bank. These are controlled by central co-operative bank. These banks are formed for serving the needs of weaker sections of society like farmer. These banks are formed with intension to help underprivileged and poor people.

<u>Rural Banks: -</u> Earlier many banks were not interested to operate in rural area but due to government effort now they are the regional rural bank which do operate in rural areas and are responsible for rural development.

NABARD: - National bank for agriculture and rural development. This bank has played a key role in rural development. There are lots of scheme offered by NABARD to farmer and agro business enterprises and a lot of subsidies are too offered.

The NABARD website gives you a lot of information about new items, a brief knowledge about project and basic project report of every agricultural project. The bank have a proper procedure to give you loan and it depends upon what type of project you have.

The project report must be studied carefully; the project report contains the basic understanding about project. Among the agro business enterprises the bank is famous for subsidy, and thousands of people have taken facilities from the bank.

The readers are requested to study to the NABARD web site in order to have a good knowledge. Even if you are not planning to do business still it will give you a lot of knowledge. The web site is really good and serves as better learning exploration.

Financing by shares

Financing by issue of equity shares is very common for company. The private limited company cannot offer its shares to public but a public limited company can. The examples of public limited companies are Reliance, Tata, and Mahindra etc.

The shares are generally offered through stock exchange. The market has its own regulator called SEBI (Securities and exchange Board of India). The SEBI gives the guidelines to offer shares to public, which is required to be followed strictly. Due to various frauds committed by the companies, the governments have made very strict laws to monitor the same.

The equity shares financing is a very unique way of financing, which does not require any interest and principal repayment obligation. The only remedy available to shareholders is to sell shares in the stock market. The share holders are free to sell then at shares market at any time.

The shares are generally at the face value of Rs 1 tots 100 and offered to public at the premium price i.e. price above the price of the shares. The premium amount could range from Rs1 to 1000 or even more,

Let it understand by an example the share price is Rs 1000 which is composed of Rs1 towards the face value of share and Rs 999 towards the premium amount.

Agriculture as a Business

How do you think for agriculture as a business, take few minutes to think, you may think "it is a not my cup of Tea", people may say it required lot of hard work but it's all myth, the agriculture is a very profitable business and agriculture processing is the most profitable business to do.

Let's understand it with an example of cotton cultivation:

The estimated cotton yield in 1 acre of land in Indian (As calculated for different soil type) is supposed to be the 8 quintal to 20 quintal.

The expenses for production will estimated to be as follows for 1 acre

- Seeds cost Rs 1000,
- Fertilizers cost Rs 3600,
- Labor cost Rs 600
- Rs 500 is for irrigation of pesticides'
- Rs 500 is the labor cost for picking up the crops

so it amounts to hardly Rs 6200 in totality and you will be surprised that cotton will yield sale price of Rs 4000 per quintal. therefore for the production of 10 quintal it will fetch Rs.40,000 and profit will be =40000- 6200 i.e. Rs. 33,800 in a span of months only. It is openly left to you to make all types of calculation and decide in which business it is possible to get same quantum of returns.

One can calculate all the possible way by changing the soil conditions and different estimation but surely he will end upon profit, the only exceptions are natural or artificial calamity. Still in case of natural calamity the government compensates the farmers.

Agriculture is one of the oldest practices known to mankind. The agriculture had made it possible for survival of mankind on this planet. The well cooked food can be provided as food to infants and aged people so that they could live long and healthy. It had reduced our dependent the hunt and avoided riskier incident of life. For doing hunting and fishing you need to have good physical abilities and favorable age.

The agriculture not only provided food to mankind but also to our domestic animals like cow, dogs, pig, goats and chicken. It is also responsible for flourishing of milk industry and meat industry. The agriculture is also saving our forest as it provides fodder to our domestic animals.

Agriculture is supporting not only our economy but also social life and providing means of livelihood to half of population of our country.

Earlier people while practicing agriculture used to grow food for themselves and their family, later they tried to earn money by trading agricultural produce. With the advent of laboratories and machinery, the agricultural production has been doubled in few decades. The newly developed fertilizer and irrigation equipment made it possible to yield more out of soil.

Let go for types of Agriculture

1. Plantation of woods like Teak and other used in the making of furniture. It has a long gestation period for getting payback, but it is a big return on small investment. The plantation can be seen in many areas of our country according to suitability of environmental condition it can be practiced.
2. Cash crops like cotton and soybean can be planted for getting payback in few months, commercial crop like rubber and jute can also be used.
3. Plantation of medicines and herbs for ayurvedic and other medical purposes.
4. Agriculture of flower of selling in flower market and other costlier products like mushrooms etc.
5. Normal cereals like rice, wheat, dals etc.
6. Agriculture for animal folder like goat farming, animal husbandry etc.
7. Mixed farming for taking benefit of all the way.
8. Agriculture for vegetables and spices.

Condition of Growth: - It is different for various crops and can be made and can be customized accordingly by using fertilizer and other methods.

1. Annual rainfall required which is different for different crops and same can be compensated by proper irrigation facilities.
2. The requirement of temperature is different for different crop so before going for agriculture is should look for the required conditions.

Soil Condition: - The different types of soil condition are required for different crop the soils are like soft, heavy, hard, clay, having different moisture contain and different PH value of scale.

The health or soil is also very important factor and this would require various types of fertilizers to keep soil healthy and useful. The above conditions can be controlled and maintained by using green house (Poly House) but it is generally used for costlier crops.

The soil condition is deteriorated after taking the regular crop and hence proper use of fertilizer is required. The fertilizers are chemicals and may harm the environment in some of other way and therefore use of organic fertilizer should be preferred.

The crop is also subject to certain disease which have created the role of pesticides comes to effect but the pesticides are also type of poison and should be carefully used and stored in proper condition and peoples are advice to use environment friendly pesticide so that environment should also be taken care of.

Administration of Diseases: - The plants and crops diseases can also be controlled by various natural ways like use of predicator birds, insects and usage of diseases-resistance seeds. There are improved crop seeds which show the resistance to certain diseases and pests. The seed should be used under hygienically treated condition.

Kharif and Rabi

Crops are grown in a particular season and in India popularly known as kharif, Rabi and laid.

Kharif crops are sawn in May to July and are harvested in September to October for example cotton, tobacco, jawar, rice, bajra, maize, jute etc.

Rabi crops are sawn in cool climate in season of October to December for sowing and February to April for harvesting. The examples of crop are potatoes, gram, wheat, barely, linseed, peas etc

Laid raised throughout the year are creating artificial condition like artificial irrigation and green house controlled condition the examples are vegetables, leafy vegetables, cucumber etc.

Export of Agricultural and Animal Husbandry products:-

There is a lot of potential for export of agricultural and other animal products. The people generally have less awareness about these exports but you will surprise that India is a global exporter of agro based and other product. The Indian pickles, species are in very heavy demand in foreign country. The limb and goat meal including cow meat is exported to Middle East countries from India on regular basis (daily).

The examples of exported products are cotton, basmati rice, spices, tobacco, coffee, marine product, tea, oil cakes. Interested persons could visit the DGFT website (Director General Of foreign trade) for details. Now a days doing the exports is a very simple process.

Animal Husbandry & fishing

The Animal are old friend of mankind, we are depend upon them for milk, hide & skin and even for meal. The meat is a good source of food. The fish and prawn are also very much used by people in their daily meal. The eggs are consumed in many ways by people. Farmer, fishermen and many tribes living in hill areas and desserts are totally dependent upon animal husbandry.

The animals which are used for husbandry purpose are cow, buffalo, sheep, goat, pigs, horse, chicken etc. For the beginner, it is suggested to start the activity with few animals for a year and then go for bigger commercial activity. In meat industries now a day's sells all the parts of animals. The fact is that in developed country they does not throw anything but use every part of it for making medicine, pedigree (food for dogs), skin for making leather articles etc.

Chicken: - The Deshi chickens i.e. usually found in India is very costly and take long time to grow. Therefore breads like boiler are used for poultry business as it grows faster and bigger.

Goat: - Many people breeds goats, it take a year to grow chicken to standard size. Which could be sold, few goats get larger and used for festivals like Bakara Eid. In many countries the goat meat is eaten on large scale. The goat meat is also exported in larger amount.

Sheep's are breaded by people for 3 purposes 1) Wool, 2) Meal, 3) Milk. Its milk is contain fats and used for various purpose including beauty products.

Pig: - They are not so popularly eaten in India, but in future it may be, it is a cheap source of food and pigs can be reared in all condition and they required not much care for rearing which may develop the market for its meal.

Cows and buffalo:-The breading of larger animals for milk and meat is also an age-old practice. It requires larger space for grazing. The meat of larger animals is in great demand in Middle East countries.

Diseases: - The animal like human beings are also subject to many diseases which include viral, bacteria, fungal and even hereditary. The foot and mouth diseases are very common among larger animals so you will need a doctor as a consultant and you should personally have awareness about it.

Fishery: - The fishes and prawn & crabs can be breaded in ponds. With advent of technology of fish and other breeds can be breaded in controlled conditions so that it will grow in size and numbers. It will also free from many diseases. The prawn business is a very big and prawns are very costly food. The people now days are finding this business very attractive. The crabs are also finding their places in our food. There are lot of opportunity in their business.

Sericulture :- i.e. rearing of silkworm, which is also very popular among new business man the silkworms feeds on mulberry leaves and makes cocoon which contains silk of around 2.5 to 3.5 kilometer which is required to be unbound and extracted from warm this is a very good business for new person.

Bee hives: - The bees are required for their honey and pollination capabilities. The honey bees travel from flower to flower in search of nectar and also execute the task of pollination which helps farmer to take additional & quick production.

Fishery and marine product & water products

Now day's people are consuming marine product at large. The cosmetic industry is a big customer for fish and the other customer includes, fertilizer industry and general public find it as a source of delicious food. The pharmacy industry uses some product for the preparation of medicines. the well known example is the "cod liver oil".

The problems of Farmers

The reason which makes farmers suffer a lot is not so complicated. Basically they are illiterate and rely upon their old learned ways and traditional practices that have learned from their forefather. Earlier they are unaware about various pesticides and improved fertilizers.

Due to increasing population the land holding of farmers are getting smaller. As the holdings are getting smaller, it is difficult and uneconomical to apply machinery. Due to environmental changes the soil conditions and frequency of rains is also changing. The areas which have seen insufficient rain are now facing the problem so flood which brings the changes in soil. The excessive use of fertilizers also affected the health of soil badly.

Knowledge portal: - Earlier there was miscommunication between farmers and government sponsored agency for exchange of information about various schemes and different improvised techniques for farming. Now recently the government has launched the DD Kisan Channel and Kisan Helpline Number for the betterment of the farmers and same is working as a new path of improvement.

New opportunities and Benefits available in Agriculture: - there are lot of opportunities available in framing one most important opportunity is the contract farming, same is useful to both framers and young entrepreneurs. In This way the old farmers' and young people of India could go hand in hand by using their knowledge and experience to make farming a profitable business.

Some time people used to ask about, why the farmers are committing suicide. It is the reason is that due to non profitability of business. But when it comes to calculation we can find that the agriculture is an only business which does have margin up to 100 % or more, then why it is so.

I will take you a short tour, there is another business called pharma (medicine) which does have such margins i.e. up to 400%. They even sell a medicine for Rs. 50 which is having a manufacturing cost of Rs. 5 to 10. Then let's try comparing these two businesses. The second one is very organized and these are no wastage or waste is very little. Every product does have life of more than 15 months. They pharma companies even sponsors foreign tour for their seller.

The expert who have studied agriculture industries have come up with following reasons of farmer's suicide.

1. Many farmers does have debt which is not taken by them i.e. it is taken by their father and grandfather and that is too at very high rate 10 to 15 % per month.

2. They spend heavily on childbirth, marriages, other types of family functions

3. The lands are not artificially irrigated i.e. they depends upon monsoon rain and their income in hands of monsoon which is now suffering from global climate change.

4. Their land holding are very small and due to which it is not economical to use machines. The statistics of land reveals that their land holding are reducing year by year due to increasing family size.

5. Many farmers are illiterate and due to same they do not aware about new variety of seeds, modern technology and new method of agriculture and therefore it again leading to low production.

6. Per hector production taken by Indian farmer and that of foreign (developed country) is very significantly different and we are far below their standards.

7. The costs of living are also increasing in villages and due to the same farmer are becoming more and poorer.

8. The farmers are not organized. The cooperative a society who supports the farmer has problems of their own.

9. There are lots of schemes which are provided by states central and local government to farmer but they are unable to take any advantage of it.

10. During the season all the farmer come into market with the same product. As there is no proper storage facility available to them.

11. We are the having agriculture based country and there is not sufficient godowns, warehousing, cold storage facility at all. Government is trying to establish these facilities but still there is lot to be done.

12. The tinned food, precooked and packed food is now finding places in the supermarket, but still it is not finding a place in our home. As it will take time to change our likings to packet food. The food processing industry is still underdeveloped.

13. The agriculture insurance is still a new thing for the farmers and may farmers have not insured their crops which could cost them a lot in case of calamity.

Agro based Industry

Agro based industry is one of the biggest industry in our county. We use agro based product in our day today life. The Textile Industry, Cooking Oil, Oats, Various packed food like Magi, Horlics and many more are procured by this industry.

These industries have perpetual life and as it sells product to every living being which are increasing day by day. The demand of processed agricultural product is never ending. Therefore I request the reader to start doing at least one small scale agricultural business for learning it. It could make you rich in coming years.

Agro Processing: -

It is a best choice for the entrepreneurs investing between Rs 15 lacs to Rs 250 Lacs. There are subsidies available from state/ central Government. The processing industry is a fastest growing segment in our economy. It is simple to establish and does not require super skills to start the same. The examples include, Oil processing, Dal Mill, Rice Mill, Ginning and pressing etc.

Transparency, Accounting and Book keeping

Transparency -

When we read newspaper we see few companies declaring their profit and loss account and Balance sheet in the newspapers. This ensures the transparency of the company affairs, which creates the confidence among investors.

These are the companies where public have invested heavily i.e. companies like Reliance, Tata. There are crores of people who have invested in stock market. This investor expects transparency which could be ensured by showing them the audit report of the company.

The shareholders of multinational companies are not only in India but also in other parts of the world and they want to know whether the company is making the profits and how much dividend (share of profit) they will going to get. In this way the director will report to shareholders, Government authorities, and Lenders, Creditors, Debtors and customers. So that they could judge the financial solvency of the business.

Book keeping

"Book- keeping is the art of recording business transactions in a systematic manner". A.H. Rosenkamph.

"Book- keeping is the science and art of correctly recording in books of account all those business transactions that result in the transfer of money or money's worth". R.N. Carter

The book keeping does not means the books we read,but it means what the book we write i.e. accounts books, the book keeping and accounting are not one and the same thing The bookkeeping is done for keeping all the business records. The accounting is only concerned with money related activity.

to examine it further, all the information generated in business is not of accounting use, for example address of employees their personal data and architectural records of the building are not relevant for the accounts

The book keeping is useful because it ensures systematic recording of all business transaction so that the accountability is ensured and the responsibility of persons could be checked, we can study the transaction of the business after years also.

It gives us record for complying with various statutory compliances like filing of VAT Return, Income Tax Return and other relevant compliances; it serves as the records when we have to face some government enquiry and also serves as evidence in the court of law.

It serves as the records for year so that we can do the comparison between years and understand our performance, it serve purpose of preparation of profit and loss account and balance sheet and it helps to make the reports to the management and helps management to take the timely decisions. It helps to formulate the policy of the business

It help us to understand the outstanding from debtors and creditors so that in case of any confusion and discrepancy it serve as the record for argument in the court, so one should not destroy the record unless the matter is settle.

ACCOUNTING

Definition of Accounting
American Institute of Certified Public Accountants (AICPA) which defines accounting as "the art of recording, classifying and summarizing in a significant manner and in terms of money, transactions and events, which are, in part at least, of a financial character and interpreting the results thereof".

Following are some basics of the accounting one must know

1) What is importance of accounting in business and what are their objectives.

An beautiful example can be quoted here that we all know that the banks are not opened for the whole day. The working hours of the banks are 3 to 5 hours for public, then does the banks gets closed, the answer is "no", the Manager has lot of work to do and it takes 9 pm in the night for the managerial staff to close the bank.

Why it is so, because they have to make the accounting and reporting of the day's. This is so because they are dealing with public money. Any of its customers can ask them anytime about his records. The accounting is very important because they need to report their position to head office on daily basis.

The accounting is a very important part of the business, the most important thing in the accounting that it measures the business in the money terms and anything which could not be calculated in terms of money could not find place in accounting.

For example, If Mr. A Mr. B and Mrs. C all person are doing same job and they have paid same salary of Rs 5000. Then does it men all the person are making same scarifies for the job and are they doing the job with exactly same efficiency and are they almost equally capable of doing the same job,the answers might be different and therefore accounting could not measure the personal emotions and personal problems and personnel scarifies. This is the limitation of the accounting and it is also called the money measurement concept.

Why we need to prepare the profit and loss account and balance sheet? basically in accounting the business is assumed to as the going concern i.e. it is not being the person like you and me so it will not subject to death the owner may change but the business will remain the same it may grow and scale down But the business will remain there,

The accounting for the business plays a vital role in understanding the health of the business and its future course,

The benefits of accounting are pointed below.

1. the accounting keeps you aware of payments and outstanding of your business which indicates the relationship with your parties,it is strongly suggested that when you start new business you must start accounting with paper and pen i.e. you must record your all the transactions in a register which is commonly call journal i.e. diary in accounting terms when the complexity and number of transaction are too much then it is suggested to go for the computerize accounting,which requires a qualified accountants

2. If you have computerized accounting then also it is suggested that you should maintain manual records of the basic book like cash and bank and debtors and creditors' ledger. You should take printout of books and journal every week or daily form the computer.

3. The balance sheet helps you to understand the position of the business and profit and loss account aware you about you status of affairs during the year. The final statement also helps to compare your business with the others.

4. The computer system could provide you almost hundred of reports for decision making and product pricing. These reports are provided by the computers at any point of time.

5. In near future the professionals of IT sector are also developing such software's. Which will provide the accounting and auditing solutions as well as return filing solutions. And traditional, manual accounting is getting substantially reduced in the present scenario so the future of accounting and auditing will not be different from today? The Information technology and the auditor will be required to audit the software only.

6. Now a day's people are shifting on the computerized accounting because they find it convenient but there are problems with the same also,

   • *They can be manipulative*: - They can be manipulated by any of the staff or person having the basic knowledge of computers, so other internal control should be very strong to prevent the same.

   • The creditors and debtors could form a collision with accountants and can manipulate the accounts

Management of business

The management is required to ensure the optimum utilization of available resources. The management is required for managing and coordination of Man, Material, Machine and Money.

Sales & Marketing

Product life:-The very famous concept of product life cycle is very important, which states that a product has its own life, like birth, adulthood,old age and death, the birth is its innovation then childhood when the products are established,adulthood when the product becomes a brand, at this stage the product is known by its name only. The old age arrives when the other competitor leads the race and death is compared with the lac of demands of product.

I would like to quote a famous example of Beautiful Doll which was when introduced to market was a innovation then every child demanded it and now it is even out of talks, this indicates a product has its life too.

Ambassador car was also be a good example of same now the company itself has stooped the production of the same,

So other big companies' doe have such understanding in their mind and they do estimate the life of the product and accordingly spends on its advertisement and its distribution and particular machinery,

I will quote an example here, some product which are out of demand in the foreign markets but are in huge demand in some developing markets I phone 4 and 4s are relaunched by the Apple company in Indian market because the product was in great demand in India. The foreign cars are also imported in India and people drive it with the pride. These models of cars have become the obsolete in the foreign market.

The golden rule *Marketing begins before business*

The basic points in marketing.

*Large sales targets:-*The business could not survive without sales and marketing and in modern scenario marketing is very important and unavoidable. If you want to sale the good on the large scale then marketing can help you out. The marketing is the key to large scale sales targets.

Ability to look into others mind: - The person must have good ability to look into others mind. By understanding the demands and requirement of customers we can place our product in their homes and place of work.

You must have good understanding about the customers to whom you are going to deal with, what others are thinking patterns? What are others are offering? And what better you can offer to them. Sometimes people don't know what they want, and then we have to educate them about the usefulness/ appropriateness of the product.

Communication :- The positive communication is very important in the marketing the communication can be done in many way. You must understand the basic psychological aspect that how consumers make decisions of buying the product,for example Few customers may take decision by looking it,some wants to hear the benefits of the product and few might want to feel by using it, some would like to take advice of their family and friends,some may buy it after thinking about it. Now days new class of customers who buy the product after studying it and watching its video on internet and even checking its rating on electronic media. For them if the products video is not available on internet it's a fake product. How to convince the customers of different persuasions is can only be explained by marketing experience and acknowledge.

Turnover cycle

: - Have you ever thought that why we need a working capital loan commonly known as the cash credit loan and overdraft. It is because there is a time gap between purchasing the raw material and realization of sales proceeds. In certain manufacturing business this time gap may be in years.

For example :- In the ship building business the ship might takes few years to build and so during the period the ship building company may require working capital for purchasing steel and meeting its day to day expenses.

There is also an concept of fixed cost, there are certain expenses which are needed to be paid whether we have profit or not, the taxes are also somehow in nature of fixed cost like excise duty and sales tax does not concern with the realization of sale proceed but you have to pay then as the incident of manufacture, you need to pay your employees salary and TDS payments and others liability such as monthly installment of your bank loan. Therefore you need to have the working capital in order to run your business smoothly.

We must calculate the funds we need to set aside for replacement of asset after completion of their useful life; we must also set aside funds for the replacement of assets. There no need to tell you fact that if our assets fails we might unable to produce the goods.

Why we require giving credit

The basic query may come to your mind that, Why we require giving credit? : - seriously nobody wants to give credit to anyone. Then why? because credit is required to increase the sale of the business, the loss of interest in due to credit period is very well taken care of,in the price itself and this inflation of price can be given as the cash discount to encourage the early payment.

Now why were require to sale more because we want to recover the capital as fast as we can, as we have invested heavily in the machinery, land and other assets. And the business is subject to competitions and trends.

Mostly when we start the business we are having a cool calculation in our mind but when we entered in to actual business we may face the market conditions i.e. we have to adopt the market price for our product and services.

Financial Management

Many of the my readers may have heard of Sick Industry,if you search on internet you will find that there is a law called Sick Industries Act which is made for regulating the companies which are financially sick.

The industrial sickness was noticed with the big industrial units. The surprising factor was that, their end product was also in demand and they were not facing labor problems still they were on the urge of closing and same was due to poor financial management, so the financial management is very necessary and it is very important for business.

The financial management is the management of assets and liabilities in such a way that there should be no shortage of fund when we needed them. For the better financial management we may use the tools of financial monitoring and ratio analysis. The comparisons between two accounting period could give you lot of data controlling your financials.

The financial management is a very important feature of the business. The financial management is necessary so that we can do business in much economic way and to procure funds at the cheap cost and invest it in the business to get highest return.

The payback period of project is very important, which means how many years the project took to recover the amount invested in the project. It is calculated in various ways by various peoples for example Discounted payback period which considered the interest factor for measuring the payback period etc.

Cost Accounting Department

There are certain semi variable costs which are associated with the production scale and increasing production scale. It is very difficult to estimate the cost beforehand. So in that case, they need to keep a department for cost accounting. The management also wants that information to be correlated with the market conditions therefore professional are employed like cost and management accountants.

The reason of keeping the costing department is the price is generally detected by the market. It is very important to analysis the cost structure. The scale of operations does have the strong effects on our weaknesses and strength for example if you are doing maximum of your work by your own you could save lot in small scale business,but you lose many if you are unable to take work from others. It helps to understand the cost cutting area. In a small business the proprietor have the direct control over the business therefore cost reduction and control is very easy, but in a large organization it is requires the professional and expert to reduce the cost.

What is internal control in a business?

The internal control is very important in business, as it prevents pilferage, theft and misappropriation of assets. The internal control insures that everything is going according to standard operating procedures. The separation of duties, rotation of jobs, Internal audit could be a part of internal control.

Business and mercantile laws

Following are the brief introduction of the relevant business laws applicable to the business, there may be other laws, and the list is not exhaustive and indicative in nature

Law Affecting the Business

Every person in this country when he plans for business have fear of laws, the laws are the fear factor of the business. Sometimes we think that why we needs so many laws. But the laws are very important and become one of the most important factors in this business. Earlier when you to start the business you may feel fear about the same, later once you are used to it you may understand importance of same.

Before starting the business one should not have fear of law the he must try to understand it.

The laws are as important as it insures equal importance to everyone, fair deal and human rights of the individual's. One should try to be fair & reasonable with the person under whom he is working and person who are working for his organization. The law insures the equality in society

The law ensures Bread and shelter to all underprivileged people. Law in the form of taxation collects money from rich people and spends it on subsidy and infrastructure so that the development growth of country is guaranteed. The development ultimately helps tax payer on to live with a better standard in a healthy environment and better condition and new opportunities for business.

The mercantile law includes

1. <u>Indian Contract Act 1872</u> - Few people may be surprised by 1872, but just for your information after independence we have adopted many of laws made in British. Later we have amended the same. So this is a very common law. It is basic law; if you want to read please buy Bare Act. It is very simple to understand. It is a law which define what the contract is and what are the content of a valid and legally enforceable nature. It decides what legality of the promise is. It also defines duties and rights of the parties who are entering into contract with each other. It defines coercion, fraud, under influence, offer, acceptance, consideration consent.

Agreement = offer + acceptance
And contract is agreement + enforceability

It does define circumstance under which an agreement is not enforceable i.e. void agreement and void contract. It also define implied contract. It explains the person who is eligible to contract and under which circumstances a minor can enter into contract etc.

<u>The Sale of Goods Act 1930:</u>- It is a mercantile law which defines all the basic point of Sale of movable properties. It defines buyer, seller and what goods are. One should read this act when planning for business so that he will be well aware of right of buyer and right & duties of sellers. The problems and advantages of selling goods and the law ensure that seller is not going sell improper goods to the buyer.

<u>Consumer Protection Act 1986 and amendment</u>: - This act is enacted by parliament to protect the large population of people who are consumers. Everyone knows that India is heavily populated country and millions of people are illiterate. They are even not aware of their right and privilege. So in order to ensure healthy practices of business the consumer protection act came into existence and now a day everyone is aware of it. Since enacted it had covered almost all important aspect of consumer protection and numbers of people have benefitted.

The department is also increasing awareness of people regarding act and now a day's everyone have some awareness of it. It has following objectives regarding protection of consumer rights against the goods & services which are

1. Hazardous to life of persons and property.

2. Unfair trade practices, information about quantity, quality, purity, potency, price and standard.
3. Protection of right to access varieties of goods at real competitive price.
4. Consumer exploitation, consumer education and to forbid the trade practices which are responsible for undue exploitation of consumer.

<u>FEMA Act:</u> - Foreign Exchange Margent Act is an act made for people who are dealing in foreign exchange 1991

"The law is having objective of facilitating external trade and payments for promoting the orderly development and maintenance of foreign exchange market in India."

The act is useful for those entrepreneurs who are willing of carrying export and import. The exports are desired by the country as it is useful for the development of country and earning of foreign exchange.

The act covers: - Dealing in foreign exchange, holding of foreign exchange, export of goods & services. Realization of repartition of foreign exchange, exception from realization and repartition is certain cases contravention and penalties.

<u>The Indian Partnership Act 1932</u>

This is another British adopted act which defines the partnership and separates it from agency. The law defines the privilege, liability, right & duties of partner.

A new law of LLP – Limited liability partnership comes into force recently and introduced the concept of limited liability in partnership which was there in the private and public company.

It defines the nominal partner, sleeping partner, dominant partner, working partner and their role responsibility and liability.

It gives the information about dissolution of partnership, admission of new partner, retirement, expedition of partner and alteration of partnership deed. This is very basic act for reading and registration of partnership is suggested to enforce the law in an effective manner.

It further states about duties of partners to indemnify other partner in case or fraud by partner, conduct of business, mutual rights of partner and their liabilities, property of firm, partner as a agent of firm, extension and restriction of partner implied authority, partner authority in emergency, mode of doing act to bind firm, liability of partner for act of firm, liability of firm for wrongful act of a partner, holding out, minor (below 18 years) admitted to the benefits of partnership. Incoming and outgoing partner, insolvency of partner, liability of estate of deceased partner, Right of outgoing partner to carry on competing business. Right of outgoing partner to share subsequent profits in certain cases, compulsory dissolution by court etc.

The Labour Law :-

Following are the Industrial and labor laws –

1. Factories Act 1948

The objectives of act are to ensure adequate safety and to promote health and welfare among the employee. Applicable to factories employing more than 10 workers, working any day of the preceding 12 months. It requires among other things suitable arrangement for the provisions of latrines and urinals for the workers. The total weekly work hour should not exceed 48 hours, extra wages for overtime.

2. Minimum Wages Act 1948: - This act is made to ensure that at least minimum wages as determined by government should be paid to labor to ensure his/her standard of living a humanitarian, treatment to him.

    The philosophy of minimum wages act has been explained in the Supreme Court quotation in the case of State of Kerala Vs Unichop (A.I.R. 1962 SC12)

    What is minimum wages act purports to achieve is to prevent exploitation of labor and for that purpose empowers the appropriate government to take steps to prescribed minimum wages rates of wages in the industries. In an underdeveloped country which faces the problem of unemployment on a very large scale, it is not unlikely that labor may offer to work even on starvation wages. The policy of the act is to prevent the employment of such sweated labor in the interest of general public and so in prescribing the minimum rates. The capacity of the employer needs not to be considered. What is being prescribed is minimum wages rates which a welfare state assumes every employer must pay.

This act fixed minimum rates of wages in certain employment only and not all employment.

The Payment of Wage Act, 1936:-

The act is made to ensure that actual payment of wages should be made to labor and there should no unauthorized deductions to be made. The payment should be made in regular interval and to eliminate all malpractices and illegal practices.

Employees Compensation Act – 1925:-

This act is made to ensure the social security of the employee i.e. workmen and people who's dependent on him. These acts ensure that the compensation must be paid to the workmen working under hazardous and such other type of organization. The compensation is required to be paid when injury by accident leading to death or disablement while working in Industry. It also includes certain occupational diseases arising due to such employment.

Contract Labor (Regulation and Abolition) Act, 1970

Contract labor are common in many organization including the government controlled and owned industries. Many organizations are employing the contract labor for their operation. It assigns the contact with a contact of supply of labors.

The most important factor for employer was that they don't need to provide for any retirement benefits, bonus, ESIC, EPF and many others. They were not subjected to strikes as the organization brings in new contract who take care of employer work.

These contract labors were living and working in very pity working condition, they are like a daily paid labor. They are not having any social security and it is observed in much case they are not provided fair wages and the wage discrimination is very common. They are not awarded with compensation in many cases. So government was biggest concern about them and introduced this law for their welfare and to ensure a humanitarian & respectful treatment to them.

The act is applied to every organization/contractor establishment who are employing 20 or more such worker during any day during the preceding year. The act protects the interest of contract labor in terms of equal remuneration, legal working hour, regular payment and proper legal compensation in case of injury or disablement. Other basic facilities like drinking water, toilets and rest room are also covered. It ensures protection of their health, welfare & social security.

Equal Remuneration Act, 1976:-

The act is made to ensure that the women worker is paid in equal terms as the male worker is awarded. The law ensures that no discrimination made in terms of remuneration by subject of gender only. It ensures equality among worker. The act empowers women and made them aware about their legal rights and duties.

Employee's State Insurance Act, 1948:-

It helps employee to take care of their sickness, maternity and injury in the course of employment. The government operate ESIC scheme to benefit worker. The law is applicable to the factories employing 10 or more number of labors at any day during the preceding year. Scheme is very useful to employee & employer also because it take care of difficult time of employee. So it is recommended that one should go for it.

Employees Provident Fund and Miscellaneous Provision Act, 1952:-

The act applicable to employees drawing Rs. 6500/- per month and the act are made with the motives of saving money and needy retirement requirement of funds. The act is applicable to scheduled specified industries which is employing twenty or more worker. The act is beneficial to all employees. Now a day's mutual funds and other instrument which provides the benefits of similar nature. The PPF scheme is operated through nationalized bank like State Bank of India and its subsidies. This is government implemented and operated scheme.

Payment of Bonus Act, 1965:-

The law is meant to secure the rights of labor to share the profit of the establishment they are working for and to presence sentiment of equality and uniformly. It is applicable to certain establishment only.

Payment of Gratuity Act, 1972:-

Gratuity is a sum of money paid to employee after his/ her retirement as recognition of his services during his life time. In case of death of employee it is paid to his legal heir or nominee. It is an instrument of social security. It is applicable to establishment employing 10 or more employee on any day during the preceding 12 months.

Maternity Benefit Act 1961:-

The act applied to establishment employing 10 or more persons to that employee who are not covered under ESIC act as the name suggest. The law ensures mother rights and health and won't to allow the legal protection for her natural duties. The act allows 12 weeks leave for delivery and 6 week for miscarriage. During the period they are entitled to receive actual wage plus maternity bonus.

The Child Labor (Prohibition and Regulation) Act 1986:-

The act ensure the children below 14 years of age will not be employed anywhere and the act is there to protect their childhood and to protect children from hazardous job. The act also defined the right of worker above 14 years and their working hour and benefits to be provided to them.

The Industrial Employment (Standing Order) Act 1946:-

The law applicable to the industrial establishment employing 100 or more workmen during any day is the preceding 12 months. The act is there to resolve dispute and friction between workmen and management of the establishment. The act requires the employer to clear state. The condition of employment & communicate the same properly to the worker. As the act work to resolve dispute the act want establishment to clear define working hour, leave, medical leave, holidays, shift, termination so the dispute could get resolved instantly and in a smooth manner with name of party is aggrieved.

Industrial Dispute Act, 1947:-

This act give a legal from work and clarifies government stands and with in case of dispute arising between management and worker or their union. The dispute may be for various forms and ways like retreatment, lock-out, strikes, dismissal of workers, demonstration, stoppage of work, etc. these act helps to resolve a disputes in a peaceful process. It provides power to various authorities to deal with the matter and clear the dispute in a legal and humanitarian way.

The MRTP Act 1969:-

The act is made to prevent the unfair and illegal trade practices in the business. The act ensures that the operation of economic system does not resolve in the concentration of wealth and means of production to the common detriment. It means it ensures the concept of equality and equality among means of development. The act provides for privilege of development to everyone essential resources should be such that it senses the common people.

The act prohibits the monopolies and restrictive unfair trade practices. The act is against the people who are trying to eliminate the competition by unfair way. It restricts business to charge unfair prices. The unfair trade practice can by giving misleading advertisement and also falsely representing their product or services false claims for products.

Negotiable Instrument Act 1981:-

This is one of the oldest acts still in force; it deals with negotiable instrument like bill of exchange, promissory note, hands, and cheques. The act is very good, it defines the right and duties of partner while dealing with a negotiable instrument, and it defines distance of cheques and other negotiable instrument as well as the right and liabilities of parties in case of endorsement, dishonor, payment of interest and penalties. It also defines the capacity of parties who can draw and accept the negotiable instrument it gives legal position of negotiation, endorsement, assignment, acceptance etc. It also gives validity of instrument, how to work the instrument etc.

Beside these law as have various regulatory framework specific for particular industry.

For example
For oil mill we have following regulation

1. Solvent extracted oil, de-oiled meal and edible flour (control order), 1967
2. Pulse, edible oil seeds and edible oils(storage) control order 1977
3. Vegetable oil products (regulation) order 1998
4. Edible oil packing (regulation) order 1998

Tax laws

The tax structure is divided in two broad categories viz Direct tax and Indirect tax. A direct tax is the tax which cannot be shifted to another individual or entity. The individual or organization upon which the tax is levied is responsible for the tax payment. While in Indirect taxes the incident of levy can be shifted to another person or entity.

The examples of direct tax are Income Tax, Corporate Tax, Municipal Tax, wealth tax. The examples of indirect tax are Central excise, Sales tax, Local body Tax, Service Tax.

Project report

This is the project report of ginning and pressing unit, one can find various project reports on NABARD website, Internet and other material. The project report mentioned below is for understanding purpose only and it is not the actual one. The figure are only indicative and are manipulated to keep the secrecy of original project report. The readers are advised to take advice of experts for further understanding the same.

For the benefit of readers, the relevant point which is practically important for the project is explained at the appropriate places.

Brief about Ginning and pressing unit:-

It is the well known business which can be done for the medium level risk takers, it requires the investment of 1.5 cr to 10 cr i.e depending upon size and scale. The expected profit form project is around Rs700 to Rs 1000 per bale and a plant can produce 8 to 32 bales per hour so your earnings might be Rs 1000 to Rs. 32000 per hour.

What is project report

The project report is a document which is prepared by a professional after doing very in-depth study of the various aspects of project under consideration. The project report is a formal document and it is a very important document. It is prepared to explain the following points.

- Financial feasibility
- Technical feasibility
- Future sales projection

Kindly refer the following project report of ginning and pressing plant and the above mentioned points are explained at appropriate places.

The following is the project of establishment of cotton Ginning and pressing Unit for the sake of readers. I would like to explain the basics of project.

While wearing the cloths, have we ever thought that how the cotton does makes its journey from farms to our wardrobe? At the first the cotton grower (Farmers) cultivated it in his field and then he picks it up and sale it to Ginning factory, the ginning is a processing industry.

It separates the cotton seed and cotton lint from the raw cotton (Kapas) then seed are sold separately to OIL MILL and Seed Manufacturer and farmers. The lint cotton is converted in to a cotton bale of 170 kgs by pressing the same with high power pressing machine. For the sake of covenant the readers could go to you tube and intenerate for watching the video of cotton ginning to have a good idea about it.

Then this cotton bale goes to spinning industry which is a large industry and their they convert it into yarn i.e. Cotton thread and theses threads are send to textile industry where they are colored and weaving is done and cloths are made. Then designers cut it properly to make cloths.

Project report
Ginning and Pressing of Cotton

<u>Summary of Project</u>

This project report is prepared for the establishment of Cotton Ginning and pressing plant. the ginning and pressing industry is an age old Industry. Earlier it was labor intensive till advent of new technology. The new technology had not only reduced the labor problems but also it had increased and improved the speed of production and quality of the cotton lint and cotton seeds respectively.

This project report is made with the view of establishment of a small and medium scale plant of 24 Double rolling cotton ginning machine. The plant employees a automatic bale press with the production capacity of 25 bales per/hr. the plant will be a fully automatic plant.

The Installed capacity of plant is 24 DR, where each DR is capable of processing up to 285 kgs of cotton per/hour and the bale press is capable of producing 25 bales per/hr.

The final product is the industrial raw material. The products have the ready market therefore. The factory wills sale its entire produce immediately. The product will also sell in international markets.

The demand for cotton bale is ever increasing and it is increasing in positive growth trend so that project will have a steady demand for its product in the future. The expected investment in the project is 4 crores and out of which plant and machinery is expected to cost Rs 2.5 cr and rest will be spend on civil work and factory shed.

The project will give employment to around 30 peoples and will create a good business opportunity. The breakeven point of project is 30% of installed capacity and it is having the payback period of 4 yrs.

Details of Product

The raw cotton i.e. kapas is used as a raw material in the process and the process leads to one main product and two by product i.e. cotton bale as a main product and cotton seed as a product and cotton waste.

Uses of product

The lint (Cotton bale) is sold to spinning and the cotton seeds are sold to oil mill and waste is also sold to certain traders who use it for less useful purpose.

In spinning mill the yarn is prepared from cotton bales which are further used to make clothing. In oil mill the cotton seeds are used for exaction for oil and remaining is a rich source of protein which used as the animal food. Further the cotton seed oil is used by oil manufacture for making the cotton seed oil for household purpose. **Cotton** seeds are also sold to seed processer, organic fertilizers manufacturers and edible mush room.

Selection of site for locating factory

The location of factory is very important, and it also affects your competitiveness, one should be careful while selecting the site. As huge quantity of raw material is required, the site must be near to raw material. The site may be very useful for the project but it may not be allowed by the government authorities so before finalizing the site one should go to Town Planning authorities for enquiring about site.

If you need to purchase the land for project. Then before purchasing the same, kindly get is verified from Town planning authorities and Pollution control board to confirm the suitability of site according to their rules. For instant, I would like to quote few rules of such authority; the factory must be I km away from village and 5 km away from municipal limits, 30 Meters away from High Tension wires. The most important factor is this rule are subject to changes i.e. the distance might be increased or reduced by the government. Earlier there was rule of 25 Km away from municipal limits which was reduced to 5 km by new government and god knows what will go to happen next.

Location of plant

The location is very important for working of the plant and business economy the plant must be near raw material if is a sellers product and the manufacturing activity must be near market if it is a buyer product. The proximity of source is important for the ginning and pressing unit and hence our unit is located in the cotton belt of the region.

The plant is not in the Industrial area as there is not vacant industrial plots are available and we have made the industrial NOC for setting of the plant.

The site is also an important factor; the land on which the plant will be placed must be a strong and plane so that not much expenditure will be incurred on development and leveling of it. It must be near to power source so that expenses of bringing power will be much reduced. The proximity to a road is very important; the water source must be in the land like Well or Bore well.

Distance

First take the property documents of the site (7/ 12) of site, where you want to locate your factory. Then on the next step you need to go to the relevant office i.e. The SDO/Tehsil Office and then apply for Industrial NA.

You need to visit Tehsil office and to meet the assistant of Tehsildar or SDO, they are always very cooperative, and they will guide you properly if possible try to meet the concerned officer in personally and give necessary documents in his hands by yourself, this procedure is not so complicated with the small projects and the assistant clerk will do all the necessary stuff.

Then you have to make application in their format and to attach the following documents in our region of Nagpur Tehsil

- Application for fast procedure there is slow procedure also you have mention it as fast
- 7/12 (seven copies)
- For 8 A
- Map Of Land (7 Copies)
- Adhikar Abhilekh Panji
- Bandobast Khasara
- K- Prat
- Layout map in Blue Print

If you don't have the following documents then you have to arrange them before hand because some documents like K-Prat may takes months to collect the after making the application in the following format you need to have ask them for what NOC they required to grant us the industrial NA.

The distance and vicinity of the project is also affected by the town planning and NOC Authorities so it is better to get the information beforehand. There is number Of NOC which is related to distance for example.

1. NHAI :- If the site is on national Highway then it requires the permission of Highway authority
2. Railway: - If it is near railway line, the NOC of railway is important.
3. Mines: - it is mining belt, then mining authority will grand you NOC.

4. Pollution: - The NOC of pollution is must if it is near River, shore line.
5. Forest Department: - Required if it is near forest.
6. Health Department: - It Is required.
7. Public Welfare authority NOC required.
8. Electricity Authority
9. Local Authority

Labors problems

Now a day's everyone talks about labor problems,now a days it is advisable to have machine based plant, the automatic plants and machinery is now available due to development of technology and hence the machine based plant are key to production. the laborer requirement should be kept at minimum and their proximity is a important factor. Otherwise you have to construct the servant quarters for them and then you have to maintain the latrine toilet,fresh water and other utilities for the same, and you must also be careful that their activities should not damage the plant or stock, they might cook food which isn't suitable for the cotton ginning plant, you must be careful about the conditions of the insurance cover so that the accidents in the factory could be avoided, you must study the activity of the laborer and understand the precautions enquired to be taken care of.

Market Study and Analysis

The market study portion covers the understanding and evaluation of markets in the past available consumption patterns and data. We have already studied the market in the market section of this book.

The market analysis is made to understand whether the market is in recession and demand for product is on positive trend or negative trend. The positive trend is very important for the project to survive.

In case of cotton ginning and textile industry for the Maharashtra, the commissioner of textile prepares the statistics information which shows the consumption patterns of the cotton over the time. Which is as follows?

World production of cotton stood at 26.23 million metric tons in the year 2013-2014. The leading producers include China, India, Pakistan, Brazil, INDIA, and Turkey. The Indian cotton nearly accounts for 101 lacs bale of 170 kg each of the total of cotton in the international cotton market. Since Indian cotton has good staple length, color, fiber strength and relatively lowers trash content and foreign materials; there is good opportunity to be good producer of cotton materials and compete in the international market with all the provided advantages of the current situation.

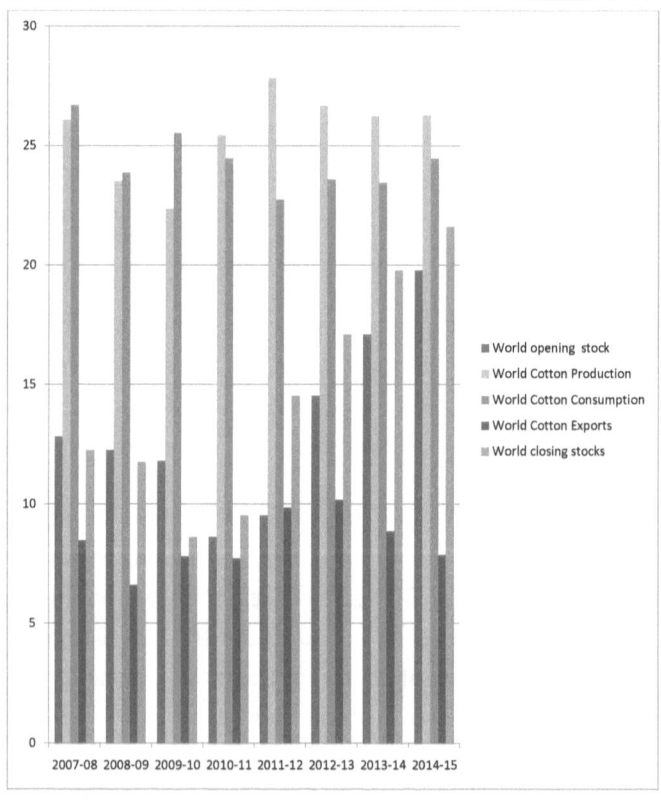

The scale

On X axix we have quantity in million tons.

One can see from below mentioned chart that area under cultivation of cotton had increased from58.82 lacs hector to 115.53lacs hector and the production of bales also increased to 375 lacs bales and advent of technology and efficiency of farmers had increased the yield of cotton crop in a tenfold growth.

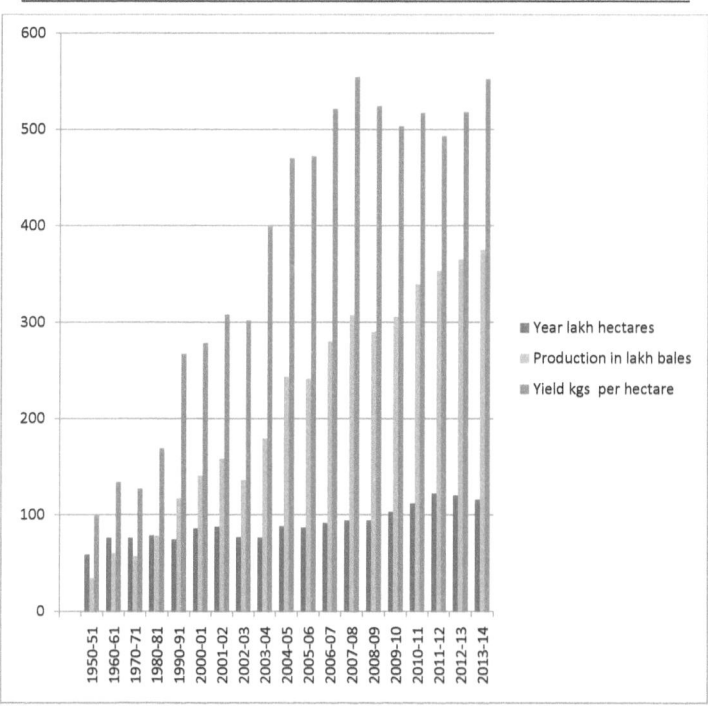

The scale
On X axix we have quantity in million tons.

It can be further noticed that the internal consumption, in India and in Maharashtra is growing on the positive trend and therefore it can be easily concluded that the Industry is very prosperous and it showing no sign of recessions but showing only the upward steady growth.

Cotton consumption by the Textile Mills State-wise

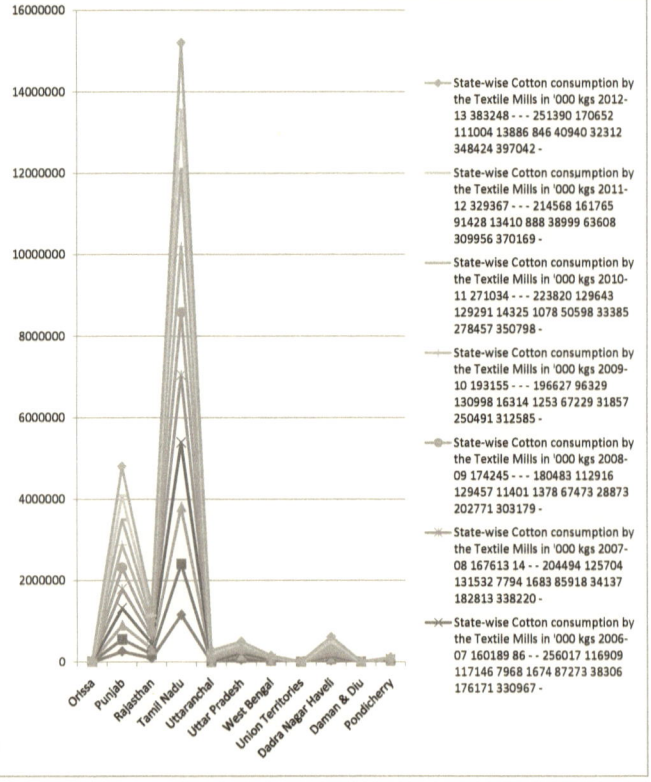

Scale on X axix is in thousands kg

Scale on X axix is lakhs of bales of 170 kg each

Cotton balance summary

Cotton balance summary

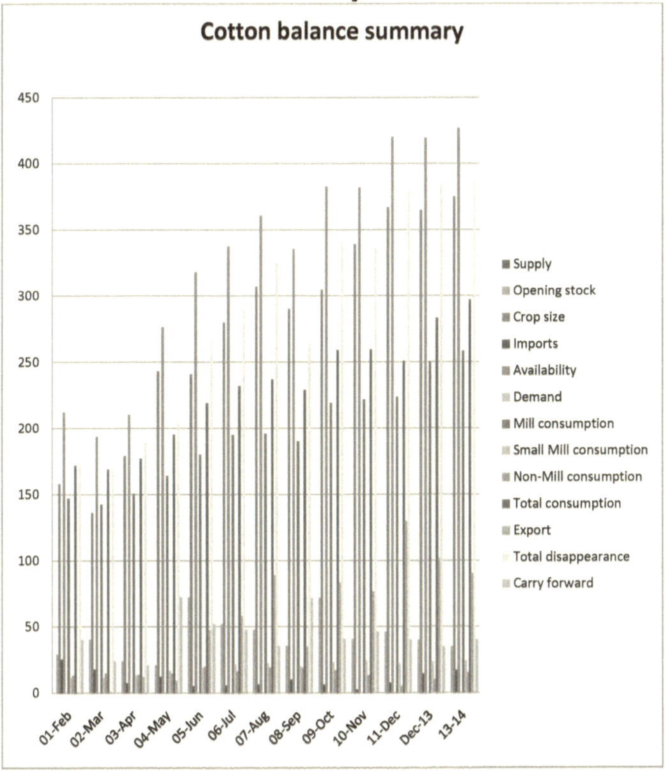

A greater attention is given to textile manufacturing and related activities in our country, a number of investors are interested in establishing many technically improved cotton farms, Ginning and Pressing, Spinning and textile industries in the Vidharbha, the prosperity in the area is guaranteed as many Ultra mega textile parks are proposed to be established in the Vidharbha specially in nearby area of Nagpur. This is help to boost economic growth of our area as well as growth of Ginning and pressing plant in Vidharbha

Along with the above the government is providing various subsidies and interest incentives scheme so as to insure that new entrepreneurs will be attracted to ginning and pressing sector and spinning and textile sectors. There is a good policy framework for industrial growth in our county and the government is taking the positive steps towards economic growth and going for lending rates cuts. These are the good conditions for establishment of new units.

Along with the above incentives the textile manufacturing industries are having various incentives from Maharashtra government too,

India has good source of quality cotton and relatively low cost labor force. All these parameters fueled the textile sector to show dramatic change in the economy of the country.

Due to the reasons listed above, the demand for the cotton textile products is quite required to cover all the demands in the local and international market.

The market segment for proposed project is 100% targeted to the international market for the last 10 years India has exported insignificant amount of lint cotton though the market is liberal for developing nations and the government has planned to export as it is depicted in the following table.

Indian Cotton exports

Indian Cotton exports

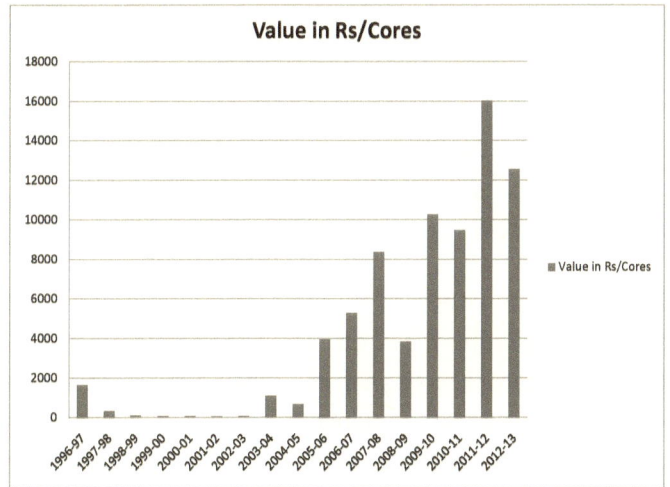

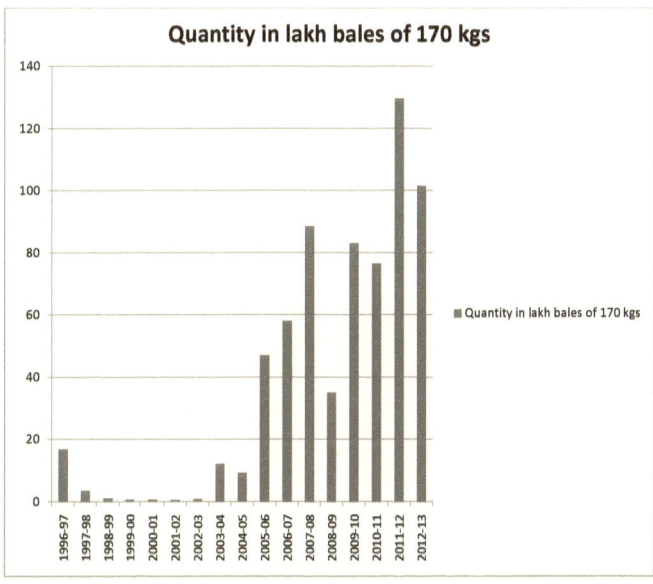

How to project the future demand

The projection of future demand for the ginned lint cotton and cotton seed, the major influential factors are export to foreign countries, growth of textile industries, agro based industries engaged in animal fodder and edible oil (refining) pressing and expansion of cotton cultivation farms in the country are considered.

As it could be witnessed by the below mentioned table that the consumptions of cotton lint and cotton seeds is increasing from year to year and this is a good indication for the business and the demand for clothing and cotton seed oil is increase in day by day and therefore demand for product is bound to increase day by day.

Cotton consumption by Orgnized and Non Orgnised (Small and Medium scale Industries)

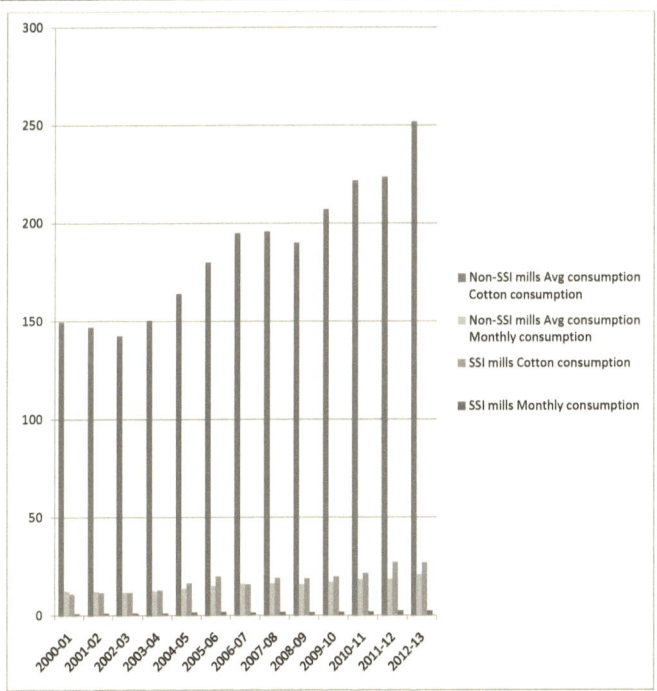

As revealed by the data set in Table 3.2, cotton bale consumption had exhibited an average annual growth of ranging from 5% to 15% during the years 2000 to 2013. Assuming this growth trend will increase to 10%, the future demand for cotton yarn is projected to range from 10% to 20% by the year 2015 and the same trend will be continue in upcoming years.

Pricing of the product and its Distribution

In our area, the Cotton Corporation of India is also a competitor in ginning and pressing industry. The CCI fixes the price of the cotton and generally it was observed that the same price is also offered by other players in the market. And based on the same, the selling price of cotton seed and cotton bale is decided. During the year 2015-16, the Cotton Corporation of India (CCI) offered the price of Rs4000 per quintal and selling price of cotton seed fluctuate between 1500 per quintal to 2000 per/ quintal. The cotton bale price was ranged between 33000 to 35000 per candy (One candy = 2 bales).

Generally it was observed that per bale net profit is Rs 1000 to Rs 2000 depending upon individual efficiency.

Prices of kapas for important variety

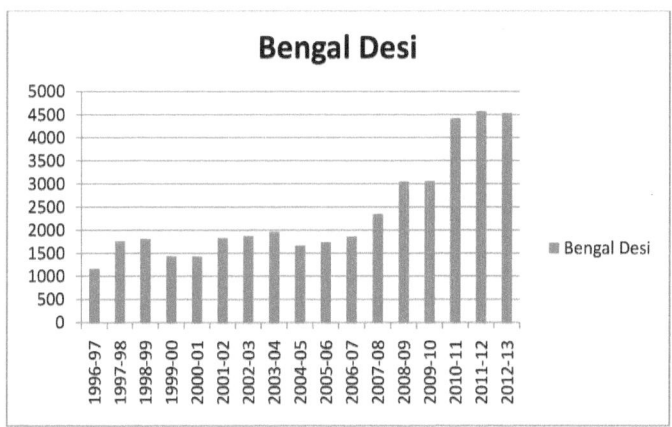

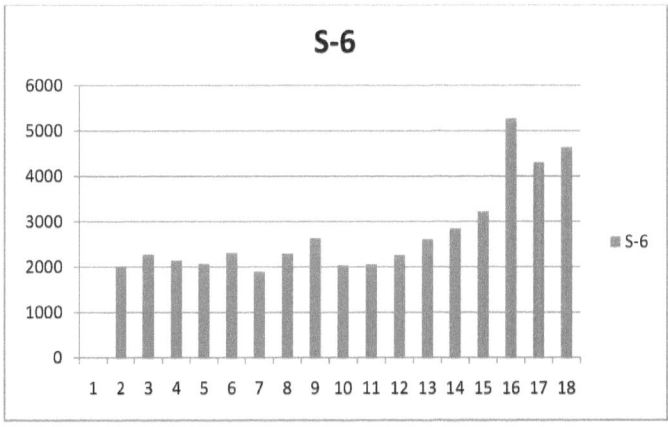

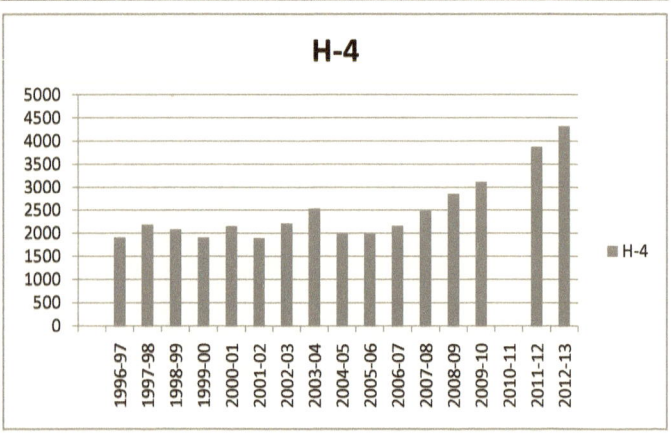

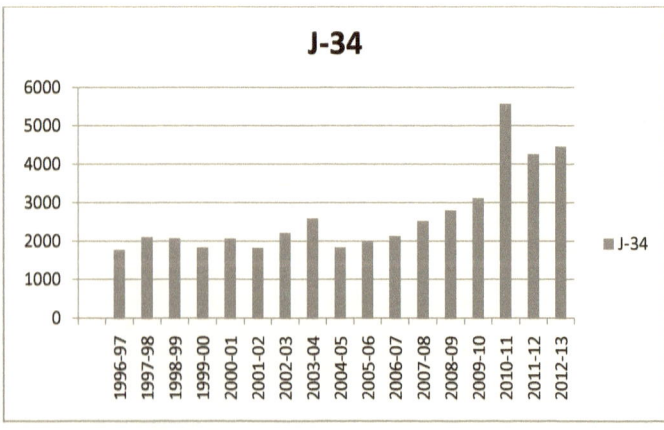

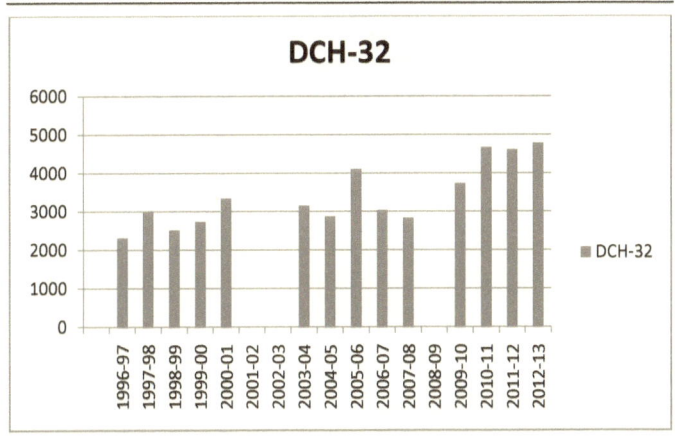

Technical Analysis of Plant capacity and production program

Plant capacity

Relaying on the projected data obtained, the double roller ginning mill is supposed to produce lint cotton and cotton seed at a capacity of 7000 tons per year. The Ginning mill will work 160 days per annum and 21 days per day in 3 shifts. The total working days in the year excludes Sundays and public holydays as well as cotton ginning is a seasonal work.

INSTALLED CAPACITY/HR	: **24 DR X 90 kgs. Lint / Hr. i.e. 2430 Kgs. Lint/ 25 Bales of 170 Kgs. Each / Hr.**
WORKING PER SEASON	: **160 Days at 21 Hrs./ Day (3 shifts of 8 Hrs. Each)**

INSTALLED CAPACITY IN TERMS OF BALES OF 170 KGS.	: **25 Bales / Hr. i.e. 525 Bales/Day for 20 Hrs.Working or 84000 Bales/Season of 160 Days.**

CAPACITY UTILISATION :

Year	Percentage	No. of Bales
1st Year	75.00%	63000
2nd Year	85.00%	71400
3rd Year	95% onward	79800

RAW MATERIAL REQUIREMENTS : 36% Lint & 63% Cotton Seed & 1% Wastage

Year	No. of Bales	Raw Cotton Required	
1st Year	63000	29750	Tones
2nd Year	71400	33716	Tones
3rd Year	79800	37682	Tones

Economy of the plant

The capacity of the plant is depends the machines like how many double rolling gin are installed and the what type of bale press our plant is using and the fact is clear that more production more profit and for getting the same you require good amount of working capital for buying the stock. The financial gearing is also a bigger factor in determination of production / sales capacity, the gearing resembles here is the amount of fixed interest bearing capital and own capital is infused in the plant

The efficiency in every aspect is necessary to meet the economy. The proposed project is commercially viable as it employing the 24 gin. It can operate in 3 shifts which insure the quick production and faster recovery of capital.

Production yield

The yield refers to how much lint we can extract from the cotton. In this industry the yield for lint cotton is expected to be 30% to 35 % and remaining contains 65 % of cotton seed and The yield of lint cotton is assumed to be 32%, cotton seed is assumed at 65% and waste is assumed to be at 2.5% to 3%.

Production Plan

The cotton ginning plant is a not so complicated in terms of technology and it does not require highly skilled labors, even an unskilled labor in few weeks training can perform well.

The 100 % production capacity can be achieved in the first year of production as well and same can be continued for next 15 years, because it is more mechanical than electronic. With low maintenance cost the plant cold operated for decades.

The Input (Raw Material and Others)

The major input is Kapas i.e. Raw cotton and same is easily available at our plant site. The area is having majority population of the cotton growers and they are very happy as they will sell their raw material locally and it will save their time and energy. Besides this the other suppliers are local traders, upcountry suppliers and also international suppliers.

Other material will be required for packing like Jute bags, packing tie wires and bale covering bags. The machinery also consumes oil at the regular interval and hence it will be required to be stored.

Other Utilities

Fuel, water and electricity are the major requirement of the plant. The following are estimated utilities requirement for the plant. The Table below indicates the details of the electric charges and lubrication charges and maintenance charges.

DETAILS OF ELECTRICITY CHARGES :

Sr. No.	Section	Connected HP / KW	Loading	Units / Hr.	Total Unit/ Season 20 x 120	Total Amt.@ Rs in Lac 10/ Unit
1	Ginning	100 / 75	80.00%	60	144,000	1440000
2	Cleaning & Automation	150 / 112.5	60.00%	67.5	162,000	1620000
3	Humidification	18 / 13.5	60.00%	8.1	19,440	194400
4	Bale Press	44.75 / 33.56	60.00%	20	48,330	483300
5)	Others	30 / 22.5	60.00%	13.5	32,400	324000
Total					4061700	

DETAILS OF LUBRICATION CHARGES & MAINTENANCE :

	Particulars	Amount (Rs.)
1	Lubrication required per season –(Gin) (0.25kg/shift x 24 M/c. X 3 Shifts x 120 days x 180 Rs./kg)	120,200
2	Lubrication required per Season –(Press) – OIL (250 Ltrs per Season x 180 Rs. Per ltr.)	70,000
3	Spares & Repairs per season _ (Gin) Rs.5000 x 24 of DR Machines	120000
4	Spares & Repairs for others	60,000
	TOTAL	**652,400**

Plants technology

Production process
Input and Feeding

The raw cotton is stored in the open space and then with the help of labor or Hoper Tractor. It is feeded to the main feeder which could be pneumatic feeder and conveyer based feeder then the feeder send it forth pre cleaning machine. the feeding system is automatic and operates on the motor. The continuous flow of cotton is very important for effective operating of the ginning machine

Gin machinery operates more efficiently when the cotton flow rate is constant.

Pre cleaning

It cleans the raw material by removing the stones, dirt, and other trash material added to it, it increases the quality of the lint and purifies the same so as to get a fair price of lint bale. The reclining device is automatic device and comes into various operations like cyclones and extractor, cylinder cleaner, impact cleaner and stick machine

Main Feeder

The main feeder is the conveyer which takes the raw cotton to the distributor machine the conveyer must be efficient and must be made of good material so that cotton should not be get dropped from it.

The lint distribution machine is the sensor based and contains sensors on the both side which indicates that machine is to when to feed to particular double rolling machine, it insures proper quantity of cotton must be dropped in the particular machine

Seed and lint separation. Double rolling machine

The roller gins pulls the cotton fibers from the seeds, the fibs are then transferred by suction to lint cleaner and the seed are send for the packing of the same, from here on words the seed are ready for packaging and sell.

Post-cleaning (lint cleaning)

The lint cleaning is very important to ensure the high quality of bales, the post cleaning cleans the lint like a washing machine but it does not use any liquid and by air only it cleanse the same, it removes the dust, small trash and other impurities

Humidification

In this process water jets are used and sprinklers spare the water on lint, this ensures the humidity of the bales. The humidity must be maintained for the expected levels and the lint must be having expected humidity.

Pressing and baling

The pressing activity is one of the main activity of the plant for the same we have installed the 25 bales per hour press, the press is up-packing press and it has two compartment one is to receive the lint and other is an alternative i.e. when the one compartment is being used by the press the others is being used to receive the cotton lint. Each bale is of 170 kgs and it is then directly sold to spinning industry where it is converted into yarn to be sent to textile for further manufacturing.

The following chart shows the process flow in the envisaged Ginning mill

Chart-1 Ginning process flow chart

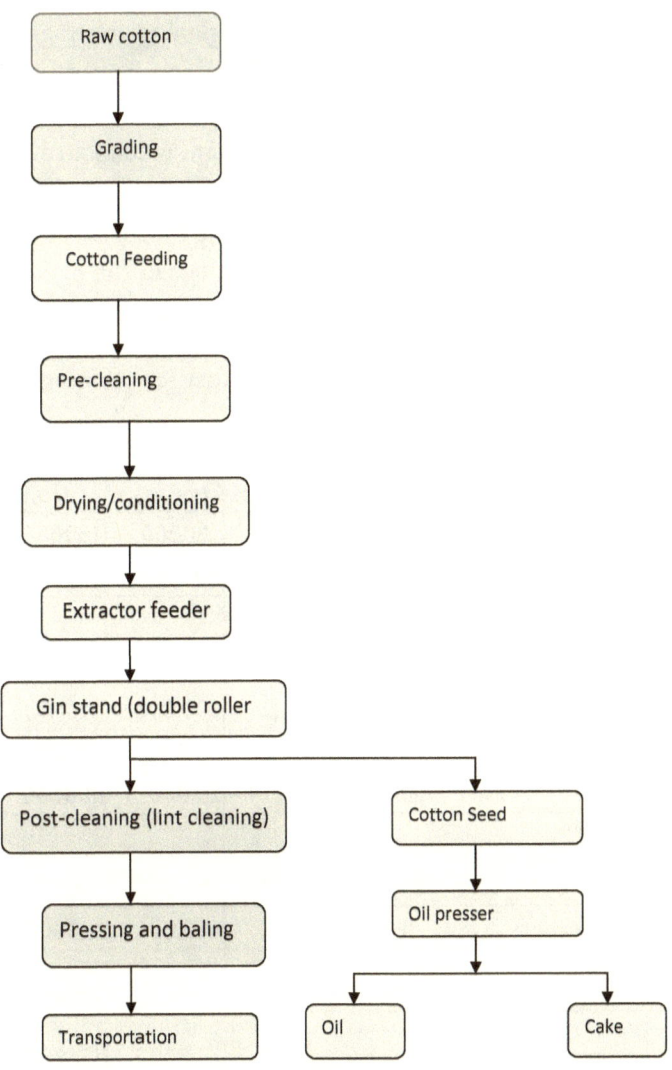

Procurement of Technology

There are very few players in the ginning machinery supply the prominent names are Bajaj and Jhadhav and many more all claims to have the state of art technology for manufacturing of machinery. The plant is suitable even for future expected production requirement and will be economical in future as well because the machineries are purchased from very renowned producer in the market with the proven track record over last decade

Machinery requirement & estimated Cost for Ginning and pressing plant

S/N	Description	Brand	Origin	U/M	Qty	Price(Rs.) U/p(Rs.)	TC(Rs.)
1	Separator	xyz	INDIA	Set	1	180000	180000
2	Dryer	xyz	INDIA	pcs	2	80,000	160000
3	Cleaning machine	xyz	INDIA	pcs	3	240,000	720000
4	Master extractor	xyz	INDIA	pcs	2	600,000	1200000
5	Distributor	xyz	INDIA	pcs	2	60,000	120000
6	Feeders	xyz	India	pcs	24	20,000	480000
7	Double Roller ginning stands	xyz	India	pcs	24	100,000	2400000
8	Lint cleaners	xyz	INDIA	pcs	2	600,000	1200000
9	Hot gas generator	xyz	INDIA	pcs	1	210,000	210000
10	Seed handling equipment	xyz	INDIA	pcs	2	78,000	156000
11	Condenser	xyz	INDIA	pcs	2	88,000	176000

12	Pressing and baling equipment.	xyz	INDIA	pcs	2	120,000	240000
13	Steam Generation unit 0.2 ton/hr	xyz		pcs	1	210,000	210000
14	Air conditioning	xyz		set	1	520,000	520000
15	Compressor GA 50	xyz		pcs	3	210,000	630000
16	Fire Fighting plant	xyz		Set	1	2,200,000	2200000
17	Electric cable	xyz		set	1	220,000	220000
18	Stand by Electric power Generator	xyz		pcs	1	120,000	120000
19	Mechanical Workshop	xyz		set	1	510,000	510000
20	Electrical and Electronic workshop	xyz		set	1	520,000	520000
	Misc.	xyz		set	1	1,120,000	1120000
	FOB Price					8,006,000	13,292,000
	Freight, Insurance, customs & Bank charges, Material handling cost					600,000	600,000
	Total CIF Land cost						**13,892,000**

Land, building and civil work

The land requirement are also subject to the sanction and limitation of NOC and town planning department ideally 3 acres of land is sufficient for the ginning and pressing plant of 48 DR, The cost of civil work and shed and building work is depends upon the individual case, as people could also build the storage facilities and construction works are different for different project

Man power and training requirements
Man power requirement for operation

EMPLOYMENT :

Ginning & Pressing process shall require Skilled & Unskilled workforce on seasonal period; Whether Administrative Staff shall be required for the year round.

Manpower Required At Ginning & Pressing factory per shift :

A) Unskilled Workforce			No. of Persons	
I)	Ginning House (3 x 3 Shifts) (18 Gins + Auto feeders)	:	3	Nos.
2)	Raw Cotton Suction (3 x 3 Shifts)	:	3	Nos.
3)	Lint Conveying in Pala House (6x3 Shifts)	:	3	Nos.
4)	Baling Press (4x 3 Shift)	:	4	Nos.
5)	Cotton Seed Handling (2 x 3 Shifts)	:	2	Nos.
6)	Cleaning – (Ix 3 Shift)	:	I	Nos.

B) Skilled Workforce				
7)	Supervisor (1 x3 Shifts)	:	1	Nos.
8)	Maintenance Engineers (1 x 3 Shifts)	:	1	Nos.
9)	Accountant	:	1	No.
10)	Manager	:	1	No.
	Total		**20**	**Nos.**

8. Financial Analysis

The ratio analysis is used for financial analysis of the project, the various ratios are used for understanding the various angle and dept of financial statement, and the ratios are further used for interfirm comparison and comparison with the industry

M/s XYZ PVT LTD

[Rs. in lacs]

Particulars		I YEAR	II YEAR	III YEAR	IV YEAR	V YEAR
Net Sales	Rs	1200.50	1500.60	1700.80	2001.20	2201.50
Profit Before Tax	Rs	40.50	50.45	59.94	74.85	85.06
Net profit/ loss [PAT]	Rs	28.35	35.32	41.96	52.40	59.54
Operating Profit	Rs	75.50	80.45	85.69	93.60	96.56
PBDITA	Rs	107.50	109.35	112.05	117.45	118.40

PBDITA / Net Sales	%	8.95	7.29	6.59	5.87	5.38
PAT / Net sales	%	2.36	2.35	2.47	2.62	2.70
PAT / TNW	%	23.95	22.98	21.45	21.12	19.36
PBT / TTA	%	7.67	8.93	10.19	12.14	13.39
PBDITA / TTA	%	20.35	19.37	19.05	19.05	18.63
PBT / Net sales	%	3.37	3.36	3.52	3.74	3.86
Operating Profit / TNW	%	63.79	52.35	43.80	37.74	31.39
Operating Profit / Net Sales	%	6.29	5.36	5.04	4.68	4.39
ROCE	%	20.35	19.37	19.05	19.05	18.63
Current Ratio		1.56	1.43	1.51	1.59	1.68
Net Working Capital		89.35	93.57	122.25	153.07	182.37
PBDITA/ Interest		2.99	3.53	4.15	5.87	9.11
Cash Accruals		59.35	63.22	67.07	74.99	79.88
Recv. To Gross Sales	days	67	61	61	58	57
Inv+Recv/ sales	days	73	73	74	71	70
S. Crs. To Purchases	days	3	18	21	21	21
Sales / Current Assets		4.81	4.79	4.70	4.84	4.87
Sales / Fixed Assets		4.30	5.98	7.53	9.84	12.03

Paid up capital		90.00	118.35	153.67	195.63	248.03
Tangible Net Worth		118.35	153.67	195.63	248.03	307.57
TTL/TNW [Debt/ Equity]	%	2.11	1.24	0.78	0.44	0.19
NWC / Current Assets [%]	%	35.83	29.84	33.75	37.06	40.31
S.Creditors / Current Assets [%]	%	4.01	22.32	24.84	26.63	26.53
Inventories to net sales (days)	days	6	12	13	13	13

COMPUTATION OF WORKING CAPITAL REQUIREMENTS

OPERATING STATEMENT

| Name: | **M/s XYZ PVT LTD** |

[Rs. in lacs]

	1	2	3	4
A. Gross Sales				
[i] Domestic	1200.00	1500.00	1700.00	2000.00
[ii] Export				
Add other revenue items	0.50	0.60	0.80	1.20
Total	1200.50	1500.60	1700.80	2001.20
B. Less Excise				
Deduct any other items				
C. Net Sales -[item 1 - item 2]	1200.50	1500.60	1700.80	2001.20

D. % rise [+] or fall [-]in net sales as checked to last year [annualized]	NA	25.00%	13.34%	17.66%
E. Cost of Sales				
i] Raw materials in the process of manufacture	1098.00	1404.00	1579.50	1872.00
[a] Indigenous	1098.00	1404.00	1579.50	1872.00
ii] Other spares	0.00	0.00	0.00	0.00
iii] Power & fuels	6.00	7.50	8.50	10.00
iv] Direct labor [wages]	6.00	6.50	7.00	7.50
v] Other mfg. Expe.	1.00	1.25	1.50	2.00
vi] Depreciation	35.00	31.50	28.35	25.52
vii] SUB-TOTAL [i to vi]	1146.00	1450.75	1624.85	1917.02
	0.00	0.00	0.00	0.00
Sub-total	1146.00	1450.75	1624.85	1917.02

M/s XYZ PVT LTD				
	1	2	3	4
	0.00			

x] Cost of Production	1146.00	1450.75	1624.85	1917.02
xi] Add: Op.Stock of F.G.	0.00	30.00	70.00	85.00
Sub-Total	1146.00	1480.75	1694.85	2002.02
xii] Deduct: Cl. stock of F.G.	30.00	70.00	85.00	95.00
xiii] Sub-Total [cost of sales]	1116.00	1410.75	1609.85	1907.02
F. Selling, Genl.& Admn. Expenses	3.00	3.00	3.50	3.50
I. SUB-TOTAL	1119.00	1413.75	1613.35	1910.52
J. Op.Profit before Interest	81.50	86.85	87.45	90.68
K. Interest	36.00	31.00	27.00	20.00
L. Op.profit after Interest [	45.50	55.85	60.45	70.68
M. [i] Add other non-op. income				
[a] Consultancy And Legal Charges	1.00	1.00	1.25	1.25
Sub-total [income]	1.00	1.00	1.25	1.25

	0.00	0.00	0.00	0.00
[iii] Net of non-op. income/exp	1.00	1.00	1.25	1.25
N. Profit before tax/loss	**46.50**	**56.85**	**61.70**	**71.93**
O. [a] Provision for taxes	13.95	17.06	18.51	21.58
P. Net Profit/loss	**32.55**	**39.80**	**43.19**	**50.35**
Q. [a] Equity dividend				
[b] Dividend Rate				
R. Retained Profit [14-15]	32.55	39.80	43.19	50.35
S. Retained Profit/Net Profit[%]	100.00	100.01	100.00	100.00

ANALYSIS OF BALANCE SHEET

Name: **M/s xyz pvt ltd**

As per Balance Sheet as at: [Rs. in lacs]

LIABILITIES	1	2	3	4

CURRENT LIABILITIES	1	2	3	4
Short-term borrowings from				
From Bank	150.00	150.00	150.00	150.00
Sub-Total [A]	150.00	150.00	150.00	150.00
Sundry Creditors [Trade]	5.00	45.00	65.00	70.00
Sub-Total [B]	5.00	45.00	65.00	70.00
TOTAL CURRENT LIABILITIES	155.00	195.00	215.00	220.00

M/s xyz pvt ltd				
	I	2	3	4
Other long term liabilities	250.00	191.00	152.61	108.43
TOTAL TERM LIABILITIES	250.00	191.00	152.61	108.43
TOTAL OUTSIDE LIABILITIES	405.00	386.00	367.61	328.43
NET WORTH				
Ordinary share capital	100.00	132.55	172.35	215.54
Surplus(+) or Deficit(-) in Profit & Loss Account.	32.55	39.80	43.19	50.35
NET WORTH	132.55	172.35	215.54	265.89
TOTAL LIABILITIES	537.55	558.35	583.15	594.32

M/s xyz pvt ltd

FUNDS FLOW ANALYSIS

[Rs. in lacs]

	2	3	4
	[1]	[2]	[3]
SOURCES			
Net profit	39.80	43.19	50.35
Depreciation	31.50	28.35	25.52
Increase in capital	32.55	39.80	43.19
Decrease in			
Fixed assets	35.00	31.50	28.35
TOTAL	**138.85**	**142.84**	**147.41**
USES			

Decrease in term liabilities	59.00	38.39	44.18
Increase in			
Depreciation Adjustment	35.00	31.50	28.36
Others	32.55	39.80	43.19
TOTAL	**126.55**	**109.69**	**115.73**

M/s xyz pvt ltd

	2	3	4
Long Term Surplus/ Deficit	12.30	33.15	31.68
Increase in current assets	52.30	53.15	36.68
Increase in current liabilities other than bank borrowing	40.00	20.00	5.00

INCREASE NET SALES	300.10	200.20	300.40

Break-up			
Increase in Finished Goods	40.00	15.00	10.00
Increase in Receivables			
Domestic	10.00	35.00	25.00
Increase in other current assets	2.30	3.15	1.68
TOTAL	52.30	53.15	36.68

Financial Evaluation

I. Profitability

As per the CMA data shown above the project is profitable form the first year and it will continue and increase in the coming years, this clearly indicates that the project is very viable and financially feasible

Payback Period

Investment cost and income statement projection are used in estimating the project payback period. The projects will payback fully the initial investment less working capital in3.8 years.

Breakeven Analysis

The breakeven point of the projects is given by the formula:

BEP = Fixed Cost/ Sale –Variable Cost.

The project will break even at 28 % of capacity utilization

Economic and Social Benefits and Justification

The project will help to bring the investment in the backward area and the livelihood of people will be improved. The plant will provide employment to 30 peoples and indirect employment to many people. Based on the presentation and analysis, one can understand that the proposed project possesses wide range of benefits that complement the financial feasibility obtained earlier. The envisaged project promotes not only socio-economic goals and objectives stated in the growth but will provide revenue to government in the form of Indirect taxes like VAT / GST and Income Tax.

www.ingramcontent.com/pod-product-compliance
Lightning Source LLC
Chambersburg PA
CBHW032014170526
45157CB00002B/697